What readers said about the original book:

"Once in a while one comes across a book which effectively 'stirs up the gift within' and unmistakably bears the imprimatur of the Holy Spirit of God. Paul E. Billheimer in **Destined for the Throne** has given the evangelical world such a book. One cannot read the author's insights without being challenged and blessed. Buttressing his discussion with Scripture, he has brought us things 'new and old,' but with a freshness which puts flesh in its place, and puts Christ on the throne."

Lee Fisher, Billy Graham Association

"This book is not for those satisfied with cradles and pacifiers. But for others yearning to be more useful in our Master's service, here is a meaty volume of practical value. It is lucid, perceptive, and alive. Too many authors merely "saw sawdust." But not this one. After reading **Destined for the Throne** one may well want to keep it near for easy reference."

S. I. McMillen, M.D., Author.

"This book challenged me to see the Church in all her glory: where we have originated, where we are going in God's eternal purposes. It ties intercession into the why of our existence. I was left with a desire to be who I am in Christ. The current renewal of the Church could do with some deepening in the areas of intercession, and I believe this book could play a part in that."

Malcolm Smith, Bible teacher.

DESTINED
TO SHARE THE
THRONE

"And they sung a new song, saying, Thou art worthy to take the book, and to open the seals thereof: for thou wast slain, and hast redeemed us to God by thy blood out of every kindred, and tongue, and people, and nation; and hast made us unto our God kings and priests: and we shall reign on the earth."

— Revelation 5:9–10 (KJV)

DESTINED
TO SHARE THE
THRONE

by
RUTH BILLMAN

Easy English Edition of
Paul E. Billheimer's classic
DESTINED FOR THE THRONE

CHRISTIAN LITERATURE CRUSADE
Ft. Washington, Pennsylvania 19034

CHRISTIAN LITERATURE CRUSADE
U.S.A.
Box 1449, Fort Washington, PA 19034

ISBN 0-87508-032-4

Printed in Colombia

To My Wife

For her valuable assistance, not only in transcribing the manuscript, but also in offering valid criticism and appropriate suggestions, this little volume is affectionately dedicated.

My Thanks to

Miss Frances Ashwell, Mrs. Howard Boardman, Mrs. Kellogg Maddox, and Mr. John Weekley for their dedication in typing and reproducing the manuscript for publication.

(From the original book)

CONTENTS

Given to Adam: Controlling the Earth • The
Failure of Adam and the Wreck That Resulted •
Looking for a Match and More Than a
Match for the Enemy • The Problem Taken
Care Of: The Birth of Jesus • It Was Necessary
That Jesus Be Born Without a Human Father •
It Was Necessary to Be Perfect • Jesus, as a
Man, in Battle With Satan • The Struggle of
the Ages • Tried in the Desert • Gethsemane •
To Understand His Suffering • Satan Beaten and
Whipped • Notes

PREFACE

No system of teaching, even religious teaching, is so perfect that it will be accepted by all. We can understand this by looking, for instance, at the teachings of Calvinism and Arminianism. The Calvinists believe that once you are saved, you will always be saved. The Arminians believe that you will no longer be saved if you fall into sin. Each of these systems has those who defend it as well as those who oppose it. Yet there are large groups of people who admit that both systems of teaching have value.

The worlds that God has made are too great to be explained by a simple, single teaching. Each teaching, by itself, fails to explain fully the reason for being. Science, helpful as it is, is of little use here. Apart from the Bible, the worlds and all they contain are a mystery. Except for the Bible there are no answers to these questions: "Who is man?" "Why is he here?" "What is the meaning of life?"

Many of the teachings in this book amazed the writer himself as he began to understand them. Do not be surprised, therefore, if the views amaze you to begin with. I would urge the reader to carefully consider the teachings from the light of both Scripture and reason.

Wherever the messages from these chapters have been given, in churches or person-to-person, they have been well received. I believe these messages are especially helpful for our times. The book is written with a prayer that it will strengthen the spiritual life of the Body of Christ.

The writer feels that many of the truths were given directly by the Holy Spirit through the Word. For this reason, they are not only his. These are truths for the Body of Christ and may be freely used by Christians, being subject only to the copyright laws. They belong to the Body.

FOREWORD

(from the original book)

I have just read the manuscript of Paul E. Billheimer's book *Destined for the Throne*, and have been inspired and challenged by the insights and fresh interpretations of the Scriptures regarding prayer, praise, and the Church's place in the world. Every Christian who feels impelled to find a deeper dimension of Christian witness should not only read this book, but study it prayerfully, and apply its principles to his life.

BILLY GRAHAM

INTRODUCTION

What is the purpose of the world and its workings — the universe? I believe the one purpose in all heaven and earth is the production and preparation of a Bride for the Son. Since she is to share the throne of the universe with her heavenly lover and Lord (as an equal) she must be trained, educated, and prepared for her queenly position.

Because the crown is only for those who overcome (Revelation 3:21), the Church (later to become the Bride) must learn the art of spiritual battle. She must learn to win the fight against evil forces. This is necessary before she can take her place on the throne. She takes this place following the Marriage Supper of the Lamb. How can she learn this art? In His great wisdom, God set up the program of believing prayer. His first purpose for prayer was not to get things done. Prayer is His way of giving "on-the-job" training for overcoming the wicked forces which oppose Him and His people. The world is a school where those destined to share the throne are trained in a practical way. The prayer closet is the place which produces the overcomer.

This means that saved humans are of higher rank than all other beings that God has made. Angels are made, not born. Christians are made, but they are also born; that is, they share the nature of God Himself. Through the new birth a person becomes a true part of the family of God. By doing this, God has lifted His followers to such a height that He can lift them no higher. David lifts his soul in high praise as he considers these truths. Psalm 8:5: "You made man a little lower than the angels."

The Church, because she has been raised with Christ, is already on the throne. This is her lawful position. Through her use of the weapons of prayer and faith, she holds the balance of power in world affairs even now. In spite of her weaknesses, the Church is the mightiest force for civilization in the world today. There is no other force that opposes the total rule of Satan over our fair world. If Satan were not opposed, if he were not held back in any way by the strong prayers of the Christians, the world would become a sorry sight. "You are the salt of the earth. . . . You are the light that gives light to the world" (Matthew 5:13–14*). Yes, the Church has a cleaning and keeping influence on the world. If this were not so, civilization would come to an end. The fact that the social order has not been completely lost proves that a part of the Church is already ruling with Christ. She is busy with her on-the-job training. She is being prepared for her place of ruling with Christ in the next world.

The Church, by virtue of her faithful use of prayer, holds the balance of power not only in world affairs, but also in the salvation of man. There is, certainly, such a thing as free moral choice. However, by the right kind

---

*Bible quotations are from *The Everyday Bible* unless otherwise indicated (see copyright page).

of praying (strong and caring) the Christians can send forth the Holy Spirit upon a soul. Then the Holy Spirit (a lover of souls) begins His work. He does not give up easily. Sooner or later a sinner finds it is easier to yield than to continue his battle.

God does not do things without the Church. This is because He is trying to bring the Church up to a higher level so He and His people can work together. John Wesley agrees with this when he says, "God does nothing but in answer to prayer."

In order to enable the Church to overcome Satan, God entered the stream of human history when He sent His Son to the world. As Man without sin, Jesus overcame and destroyed Satan. All that Christ did, He did for the good of the Church. He is "head over everything for the Church" (Ephesians 1:22). His victory over Satan is put to the account of the Church. Jesus won a victory, full and complete, over Satan. Yet God allows Satan to carry on a certain kind of warfare. God could put Satan away completely, but God is using Satan to give opportunity for on-the-job training for the Church.

Prayer is not begging God to do something He would rather not do. Prayer is not trying to change His mind. Prayer is commanding the victory of Christ to show itself. It is putting the decisions of heaven into effect on earth. Calvary destroyed Satan; Satan has no more rights on this earth. However, to see this in a practical way, the Church has something to do (Matthew 18:18 and Luke 10:17–19). God has given her the power of the lawyer. The Church is working as one sent by God. Prayer is where the action is.

Any local church without a well-organized prayer

program is operating a religious mill. Such people go in circles and get nowhere.

One can receive much teaching on prayer but without faith it will have little or no effect. The part that is so necessary and important is a living faith. Add to that fresh faith the practice of praise. Decide to praise, keep at it, be strong in your practice of praise. Praise is the highest form of prayer because it joins asking with faith. Praise gets faith going. Praise lifts our prayer toward heaven, up beyond the worries of doubt. Praise is like a soap that cleans out all the doubt. The secret of answered prayer is faith without doubt (Mark 11:23). The secret of faith without doubt is praise, victorious praise, praise that keeps on and on, praise that is a way of life. This is the answer to the problem of a living faith and success in prayer.

The secret of success in overcoming Satan and getting us ready for the throne is a great program of the right kind of prayer. The secret of this kind of prayer is the right kind of praise.

These teachings, and others, are explained more fully in the pages of this book.

1

THE FINAL PURPOSE OF ALL THINGS: THE CHURCH

God Is the Lord of History

Most writers of history have no idea of its meaning or purpose. They are able to record the events but they cannot explain them. Some of them even admit this. For example, G. N. Clark, in his address at Cambridge, said, "There is no secret nor plan in history to be discovered." Andre Maurois, a French writer, said, "Who made the worlds? Why are we here on the earth? I have no idea, and am sure no one else does either." Other writers also admit they do not understand the purpose or motives of the events they record.

Men of Old Times Could Not Explain the Mystery of Being

The Greeks of old times considered history to be a

circle. It always repeated itself, without any purposes as far as anyone could tell. Life was a mystery to the Greeks. Many modern thinkers say the same. They do not know the purpose of life. They do not know where we came from or where we are going. Their teachings about life are without understanding or hope.

Moderns See No Purpose to Life

In modern times a Frenchman, Jean Paul Sartre, spoke and wrote about this subject. According to him, man is alone by himself in a world without any purpose. Since we cannot know who we are, where we came from, and where we are going, since we do not understand the past and have no hope for the future, we must live for the present moment. Nothing but the present moment has meaning according to Mr. Sartre. It is no use to think of the future. Out of this teaching came the "now generation." These people cannot wait. The pleasure of the moment is the only thing worth working for. "On with the dance, let joy know no limits." "Let us eat and drink because tomorrow we will die" (1 Corinthians 15:32). This has been the teaching of a great many colleges. What is the result? Evil without limits has spread in all directions and departments of life. Crime and drugs have increased so much that danger is on every hand. All this has happened because of this teaching regarding the past and the future: "There is no hope."[1]

The Bible — The Only Book We Can Depend On

The average teacher of history has no idea of the meaning of history because he has not considered the only Book that teaches the truth on that subject. For most people, history teachers included, the center of history for any period of time is that country or state that has the most of a number of things. Is it the largest? Does it have the most raw materials? Does it have the strongest army? To most of us, when we think of history, we remember the great kingdoms of the past, important political and military leaders, and the men with the most money. We consider the Pharaohs, Alexander the Great, Caesar, Charlemagne and Napoleon as the makers of history. They also considered themselves to be the makers of history. They believed they were the central forces of history.

Calvary — The True Center of History

The world at large and the teachers of history have missed the point altogether. There is only one way to explain history that makes sense. It is the teaching of the Bible.[2]

The center of history is not the great kingdoms of the past like Egypt, Babylon, Greece or Rome. It is not the modern strong countries like Russia, China, the United States or any other country that shall yet appear. To find the center of history one must pass by all these important places just named. We must find our way to a small country and a certain hill in that country. The place is Calvary, where Jesus Christ of Nazareth died two thousand years ago. This writer offers his firm belief that Calvary is the center of history.

The Church — The Central Object of History

The Man hanging on that bloody cross was "before

all things" (Colossians 1:17, *KJV*). He was before history itself. He was the starting place of history. "All things were made through him. Nothing was made without him" (John 1:3). And the history that began in Him was and is formed by Him. It is also controlled by Him. "He regulates the universe by the mighty power of his command" (Hebrews 1:3, *LB*). It is formed and controlled by Him for a certain purpose. That certain purpose is the central and controlling fact of history.

Every event in history happens in order to serve that purpose. Nothing, no matter how small, is left out. The world and all around it was made to provide a proper place for man to live.[3] Why was man made? To provide a fit and loving helper for the Son. If man were not made in the likeness of God he could never be a fit helper for the Son. After the fall of man and the promise of the Savior, the Jewish race was born and cared for. From this race the Savior was born. The Savior came for one purpose: to give birth to the Church, and so to take His Bride.[4] Now we see that the Church turns out to be the center, the object of all the attention of the heavenly Father. In all that God has been doing He has always exercised great care for the Church.

If this is true, then all history is important to God and man. History is simply "His Story." Everything is co-operating with God in His purpose to choose and train His Church. The world has been made for this very purpose. All things are for the Church and for her good (1 Corinthians 3:21–23). As the Lord of history, God is controlling all the events, not only on the earth but in the heavens also. They all serve His purpose. They prepare the Church for her high place of ruling. This was the

(Matthew 7:13–14).

We have said that God knew this from the beginning. He knew that only a certain few would be His followers.[6] Since this is so, we understand that all His plans and purposes were for those few. He cared for their well-being. God ordered His angels to serve those few. "All the angels are spirits who serve God and are sent to help those who will receive salvation" (Hebrews 1:14). God had this special group in mind. To save them God chose to let His Son take on the form of a man. This small group is called the Church, the Bride, the Wife of the Lamb (Matthew 16:18, Revelation 21:9).[7]

The Bride — The Finished Product of the Ages

If a person wants to know the meaning of history he must look at the end of history. He must consider the end result.[8] We will look at the book of Revelation. Revelation is a look into the future. This book tells us how everything will end. As we read the last chapter of this book, what do we see? We see a great company of people who form the Bride of Christ. We see the finished product. We see the perfected, the washed, the holy and beautiful Bride. We see her joy and glory. We see her united with the Son of God at the wedding supper. We see her helping govern all the worlds that were ever made or will be made.

Why did Jesus enter the stream of human life? So that He could take the Bride to Himself.

From this blessed truth, we see that the Church is the key to understanding history. God raised up important people and placed them in special positions for the well-being of His Church. "God began by making one man. From him came all the different people who live everywhere in the world. He decided exactly when and where they must live" (Acts 17:26). From the beginning of time, down through the ages, God has been working towards one great event. It is called the Marriage Supper of the Lamb.

The Heavenly Wedding and What Comes Next

When God made Adam He said, "It is not good for the man to be alone." God also saw that His Son should not be alone. From the beginning God planned that an equal would be prepared for Him.[9] The wife of Adam was taken from his side, as we read in Genesis. In a spiritual way, we can say that the Bride of Christ was taken from Christ's side. To this day Jesus carries a wound in His side. This was the price He paid to win His Bride back from the enemy. She had sold herself to the enemy by yielding to him.

Listen to these encouraging words: "Don't fear, little flock. Your Father wants to give you the kingdom" (Luke 12:32). "He who wins the victory will sit with me on my throne. It was the same with me. I won the victory and sat down with my Father on his throne" (Revelation 3:21).

To be given a kingdom is not just a nice way to express a thought. To receive a kingdom means that one has gained a high position, a real position. It means that one has power to govern and to control. This is the very purpose God has for the Church. "Surely you know that God's people will judge the world. So if you are to judge the world, then surely you are able to judge small things as well. You know that in the future we will judge angels. So surely we can judge things in this life" (1 Corinthians

6:2–3). This is what Jesus meant when He said, "I have given these people the glory that you gave me. I gave them this glory so they can be one, the same as you and I are one" (John 17:22).

This matter of governing and ruling is a real thing. The Church (the Bride) is to sit with Jesus on His throne (His high place). The position Jesus has is a high position, of great importance. There is none higher. The Bride will join Him in this. "If we are God's children, then we will receive the blessings God has for us. We will receive these things from God together with Christ. But we must suffer as Christ suffered, and then we will have glory as Christ has glory" (Romans 8:17). Neither the Son nor the Bride will do anything alone.

Why did it please the Father to give the kingdom to this small special group? Why did Christ choose to share His kingdom with the saved ones? We may not be able to answer these questions, but one thing we know. God chose to do this. It gives Him pleasure.

Everything that happens before the Marriage Supper of Jesus the Lamb is to prepare for this great event. After that wedding God will really begin His great work, His plan. It is a mystery that is yet hidden from our eyes. Right now God is busy preparing and perfecting the Bride. Surely God is the Lord of history!

NOTES

1. There is a teaching about the past that says, "No one can know what happened before our time." There is a teaching about the future that says, "There is no hope." We often see these ideas in modern books. In his book *Chance and Necessity*, Jacques Monod, a French writer, expresses this. In his opinion man is just the result of a great many atoms joining together, all by chance. He explains the wonder of man by two words: chance and need. Monod believes that man is alone (as far as a greater being is concerned) and so man came into being only by chance. Monod also teaches that man has no purpose or reason for being. The same is true of duty — there is no such thing, according to Mr. Monod. In his book *Back to Freedom and Dignity*, Dr. Francis Schaeffer says about Monod, "He believes that man is a product of the unknown, time and chance" (paraphrased).

If these teachings are true, then man is of no more value than any other thing in this world. Then there is no difference between cutting down a tree and killling a man. If they are the same, their future is also the same. Of what value, then, is man? According to Dr. Schaeffer this kind of thinking is what started the problems in Berkeley, California. (The students in that college rose up in hatred against the people in charge. They destroyed much property also.) It was not only the college in Berkeley that has suffered in this way, but many other colleges as well. This kind of thinking makes man of little or no value. In other words, we could say man destroys himself. When man destroys God (when man denies God, it is like destroying God) he destroys himself. The teaching "there is no God" brings about the end of man as well.

2. Erich Sauer has expressed it well: "The one who made history and is governor of heaven and earth controls the entire process. Therefore, as the Lord of history, He and He alone can explain

history. . . . Therefore the Bible is the 'book of mankind' — the key to world events. All understanding of the whole of human affairs depends upon our regard of this book, the Bible " (*From Eternity to Eternity*, page 97).

"It is impossible to understand history without Christ" (Ernest Renan).

3.   All honest and serious teachers of the Bible agree on one thing. They agree that man is the center, the most important being that God ever made. In fact, man is His reason for making all the other things. Even Nietzsche said, "Man is the reason for the world" (Erich Sauer in *The King of the Earth*, page 49).

Let us consider the Genesis account of the beginning of the world. Leonard Verduin says, "It is clear that from the earliest days God was centering in on His main interest — man. All that went before was a time of preparing, getting things ready for man. All things were put in place so that man could do his important work. Man is pictured as the crown of the entire operation of God. Everything points towards man. The Bible lifts man to a most important position" (*Somewhat Less Than God*, page 9, paraphrased).

4.   Watchman Nee points out that the Church is now the body of Christ but will be His Bride after the Marriage Supper of the Lamb (*The Glorious Church,* chapter 3, page 46, 1968 edition).

5.   Some people have questioned this idea. They have said, "Too much is built on one verse and that verse has not been considered along with other verses." They also point out that the word used for "all things" in Romans 8:28 is not the word used for "cosmos" in other places.

However, if some things work for the good of man, then all things must work for the good of man. Let me explain. We believe there is only one God. We believe that He is greater than and above all other beings. All things that God does work together; there is harmony in His actions. There is harmony too in the things God has made — the universe is a cosmos. Psalm 103:19 teaches us the same thing. "The Lord has set his throne in heaven. And his kingdom rules over everything." This truth is central in the Psalms and the prophets. It runs from Genesis to Revelation. This means that all things in the heavens and earth are one whole, they are in harmony.

If all things are under one central control, then all things (not just some) must work toward one central good, one central purpose. We are speaking now about the good of the Church.

A Bible verse that explains this truth is found in Judges 5:20. "The stars fought from heaven. From their paths, they fought Sisera." There are many other Bible verses that teach the same idea.

From this we see that the "all things" in Romans 8:28 means just that. ALL THINGS. All things work together for good.

6. The writer believes that the saved ones are so many that no one can count them. We hear, both in the Bible and other places, of "the few," the "small number" who choose to follow the ways of God. It is a matter of comparing. If we add to the number of those who follow Jesus the babies who died as babies, and even those who died before birth, we realize the number will indeed be very great.

7. The writer believes the Church includes all the saved ones from the beginning of time to time everlasting.

8. The making of cars helps us understand a spiritual truth. At one time a car was only an idea in the mind of one man. The idea has given rise to a very great business. Much land and much money has been needed for this purpose. Great machines are needed and huge amounts of raw materials. This business employs millions of men and women. All of this has only one purpose: a small car. When the first car comes off the line, the purpose of all the work, the people and materials is perfectly clear. A CAR. When we see the car we understand what has gone before. The mystery is explained. So it is with the end product God has in mind — the Church.

9. The word "joint-heirs" teaches this. "And if children, then heirs; heirs of God, and joint-heirs with Christ; if so be that we suffer with him, that we may be also glorified together" (Romans 8:17, *KJV*). The writer of Romans is speaking of a delegated equality. We have been *made* equals. We were not *born* equals, but we are (wonder of wonders!) *made* equals.

2

THE PURPOSE OF GOD FOR THE CHURCH: HIGHEST RANK

Highest Rank for Born-From-Above Humans

You have now read chapter one and the notes that follow. Yes? Then it will be clear to you that human beings are really special in all the worlds that God has made. When we say this we do not mean to lower the rank of the angels nor let a shadow fall on their glory. They are beautiful beyond the telling, like kings in their walk. They have surprising power and are wiser than the wisest men on earth. The angels rule over heavenly kingdoms. If we were to catch sight of a single one of them we would never forget it. We would not be able to describe their greatness nor their beauty with our human words. Besides all this, the angels have positions around the throne of God. They make up the court of heaven. But high as the rank of the angels is, there is — wonder of wonders — a higher rank! Let us consider the born-again ones. Any one of them, important in the eyes of the world or not, has a higher rank.

God Outdid Himself When He Sent Jesus to the Earth as a Man

When God first made man He made him in His likeness. But then came the fall of man. How could human beings again have such high rank? Well, God Himself had thought up a plan. It includes a spiritual birth process. By this process, so full of mystery, God puts some of His very own nature into a lowly human being. We call it the new birth, or we may say a person is born again. He receives a new nature, a new spirit, yes, from God Himself.

Jesus "took not on him the nature of angels; but he took on him the seed of Abraham" (Hebrews 2:16, *KJV*). Angels were not created in the likeness of God. Is this the reason the angels cannot receive of His very nature, as humans can? It is only the human being who can have God within and express Him. Of all the things that God has done, none is so full of wonder and joy as this. He has shared some of His own nature with human beings, and fallen human beings at that. In this way God has lifted man to such a high rank, even higher than that of angels.

The Angels Were Made by God — None of

Them Came by Being Born

There are holy angels. There are also fallen angels. As far as we know it is impossible for them to be saved. This is because they were formed, or made, not born. They are of another kind, not after the likeness of God.[1] They do not have the godly nature, and cannot receive it, as humans can. They can never become a part of the Bride. This high rank is set aside for the born-again ones, none other.

Listen to what the Bible says about born-again ones: "The Father has loved us so much! He loved us so much that we are called children of God. And we really are his children. But the people in the world do not understand that we are God's children, because they have not known him. Dear friends, now we are children of God. We have not yet been shown what we will be in the future. But we know that when Christ comes again, we will be like him. We will see him as he really is" (1 John 3:1–2). Does it ever say this about angels? No. But of us humans Hebrews 2:11 says, "Jesus, who makes people holy, and those who are made holy, are from the same family. So he is not ashamed to call them his brothers." To which one of the angels did Jesus say at any time, "You are my brother or sister or mother"? None. But He did say this of His followers (Matthew 12:50). This means that we Christians are all of one origin; we have been begotten by the same Father.

Did Jesus ever pray for the angels as He did for His disciples? Hear His words: "Father, I pray that all people who believe in me can be one. You are in me and I am in you. I pray that these people can also be one in us, . . . so that they can be one, the same as you and I are

one. I will be in them and you will be in me. So they will
be completely one. . . . And the world will know that you
loved these people the same as you loved me" (John
17:21–23). Did Paul ever say of the angels as he did of
the Church, that they are part of the body of Christ, "the
fullness of him who filleth all in all" (Ephesians 1:23,
KJV)? Did Paul say to angels, or to the Church, ". . . we
are parts of his body" (Ephesians 5:30)? No, not to
angels.

The Born-Again Ones Increase the Family of God

But this is not all. (We walk softly here.) We will be
surprised as we read, "But the one who joins himself with
the Lord is one with the Lord in spirit" (1 Corinthians
6:17). This union is not in words only, nor just in the
world of ideas. It is a real union, like that of parents to
children. We become members of the original family
(Ephesians 3:15), true-born children of God (1 John 3:2),
"partakers of the divine nature" (2 Peter 1:4, *KJV*), born
of Him, called the "seed" of God (1 John 5:1, 18, *KJV*
and 1 Peter 1:3, 23, *KJV*), coming out from Him. So, from
this we see that we are close, like family, to God. His
family has become larger because of us. Paul asked some
spirited questions in 1 Corinthians 6:2–3: "Don't you
know that some day we Christians are going to judge and
govern the world? . . . Don't you realize that we Christians will judge and reward the very angels in heaven?"
(*LB*).

A New Kind of Being

We are talking about a new, different and completely

"other" kind of being. There is nothing else like it in all the kingdoms and worlds that God has made. These are the beings that God had in mind when He made the world by speaking a word. This is the type of being that Paul was thinking of when he talked about "one new people" (Ephesians 2:15). It was approved in the heavenly places that this new group should become the ruling class. This great group of born-again ones would be the Bride, the Wife of the Lamb. This group is chosen to be rulers together with Jesus. They, with Him, will be in control of all things. How can this be? By the great love that God had in buying back fallen mankind and by the union of Christ and the Church, this can be and will be, glory to God!

A Family Circle by Nature

Of course we never want to forget that there is a great difference between God, the One who made everything, and the human race. Christ is the only Son who is from before the beginning of time. He is eternal. He "reflects the glory of God" and "is the exact copy of God's nature" (Hebrews 1:3). But from the very beginning God planned to have a family circle all of His own — not only made by Him, but having His own seed, that is, His own nature. "In Christ, he chose us before the world was made" (Ephesians 1:4; also 5:25–27, 32). In order that we might be included in that family circle God thought up two wonderful plans. First, He thought of making man and providing for all his needs. Second, He thought of buying man back again through the new birth. This was because "God wanted to have many sons share his glory" (Hebrews 2:10). "For from the very beginning

God decided that those who came to him . . . should become like his Son so that his Son would be the First, with many brothers" (Romans 8:29, *LB*). In other words, Christ is the first and perfect example. Those who come after are to be made like Him.

In John 1:12–13 we learn about this second plan of God — buying back fallen humans and making them His grown-up sons and daughters. It was a method, a process including both birth and growth. Little by little, in this way, God would make His family holy and like His Son. He would teach and train them in order to bring them to glory. "But as many as received him, to them gave he the power to become the sons of God, even to them that believe on his name; who were born, not of blood, nor of the will of the flesh, nor of the will of man, but of God" (John 1:12–13, *KJV*). This clearly shows two methods of birth: the one human, and the other from God. God realizes His longing for a full family circle through His Son, Jesus Christ.

Had it not been for this plan of God there would never have been more in the family of God than the Father, the Son and the Holy Spirit.

Princes and Princesses of the Kingdom

Have you ever worked in a place of business where they made certain products — furniture, cars, or whatever? Certain men, very gifted and able, work hard to produce a perfect chair, table or machine. The first one must be very fine, for the others will all be very much like it. They will be copies of the first, exact copies, if possible. Our heavenly Father works like that. Jesus is the first, the perfect One, the One to be copied. God is doing a new thing, making a new people. They will be like kings. They will be given knowledge of governing. They will be on His ruling committee in His kingdom. They will be very much like the first One, the Son Himself.

Of course we never want to forget the difference between Jesus Christ and ourselves, the born-again ones. He was not made but is eternal; yet, because Jesus experienced human birth, He recognizes us as real blood-brothers. And, according to 1 John 3:2, that is just what we are, true sons of God and therefore blood-brothers of Christ. Christ is the first One, the holy One, for us to copy. We are to be as much like Him as it is possible to be. We have received of His very nature and we are given a place or rank higher than any other being, except God Himself.

Christ is special; there is none other in His position, no one else with the glory He enjoys. Yet He does not keep this glory just for Himself alone. Jesus said, "I have given these people the glory that you gave me . . ." (John 17:22). From this we see that the children of God will share His glory, His rulership, and His governing power. They will be as grown-up princes and princesses in His kingdom.

"A Little Lower Than God" (Psalm 8:5, NASB)

Now we see that God has raised man to a high position. How could he be higher? The only higher place is in the Godhead itself. That place is for the Father, the Son, and the Holy Spirit, none other. In the Son we have been accepted into the very heart of God (John 1:18). Because of our union with Jesus we are accepted on the same conditions as He (Ephesians 1:6 and John 17:23). As true sons, having the very life of God, full blood-brothers of the Son, members of His Body, as spirit of His Spirit — how could we come nearer? This mystery has been happily expressed by Rees Howells:

> So nigh, so very nigh to God,
> I cannot nearer be;
> For in the Person of His Son
> I am as near as He.

This agrees with the praise of Psalm 8:45: "What is man, that Thou dost take thought of him? And the son of man, that Thou dost care for him? Yet Thou hast made him a little lower than God" (*NASB*).

Lifting Ourselves Too High?

What we have said so far may seem too much. Can man be so important? We must study these matters carefully so we do not lose sight of truth. Really, God has used all the words and language that should be necessary to open our eyes to the greatness of His plan for us. If the words of the Bible have meaning, we have not overstated our position. "No one has ever seen this. No one has ever heard about it. No one has ever imagined what God has prepared for those who love him" (1 Corinthians 2:9). Hallelujah!

The wonderful greatness of the plan God has for us is beyond the telling. When Paul thought of it he prayed with great feeling, "I pray that your hearts will be flooded with light so that you can see something of the future he has called you to share" (Ephesians 1:18, *LB*). Paul realized that only the Holy Spirit could give us even a tiny idea of the high rank of the saved ones. We need a faith that comes from God. Nothing else can help us understand what God means when He says "a little less than God."

Dreams?

The Bible speaks so plainly, but the meaning is so high, so beautiful, that it is hard for even us born-again ones to believe it. Sometimes we try to say it means something different, something less than what it really says. We sometimes treat the words as if they were dreams instead of real truths. In studying the Bible there is one rule: We must believe it means what it says. Unless it is clearly a figure of speech it means just what it says. The words of the Bible were meant to be accepted as they are written. God has said it, so let us believe it is true that man was made "a little less than God."

What Does Rank Have to Do with Prayer?

That is a good question. *Prayer is not just a means for God to get His work done. First of all prayer is on-the-job training in overcoming the forces of the enemy.* The world is a school, a place for learning by actual practice how to overcome Satan and his helpers. God planned the way of prayer as training for our future place of ruling in the kingdom. In this life we are learning the use of the tools He has given — the weapons of prayer and faith. Jesus, with great cost to Himself, has already won the victory. But with these weapons we can carry on and apply this victory day by day.

In the future, will there still be enemies to fight against? We do not know. But while we now are busy in the prayer closet our character is developed. This will be very useful to us for our future life in the kingdom of God. "He who *wins the victory* will sit with me on my throne. It was the same with me. I won the victory and sat down with my Father on his throne" (Revelation 3:21).

"The crown is only for the conqueror" (Erich Sauer). How does one overcome? He must use the plan God gave: prayer and faith. *The prayer closet is the place that produces the overcomer.*

NOTES

1.   Read Genesis 1:27, Ephesians 5:22–32, and Mark 12:25. Notice that God spoke of making man in His likeness and then immediately spoke of man and woman. Man, or a human being, includes both man and woman. We understand from this that God also has in Himself something of man and something of woman. In this regard, the angels were not made in the likeness of God. They are without sex. In many ways, however, the angels are like man. They have a spirit nature, they have a mind and feelings, they are moral beings and are holy.

NOTES

3

THE MYSTERY OF PRAYER

I looked for someone to build up the walls. I looked for someone to stand before me where the walls are broken to defend these people. Then I would not have to destroy them. But I did not find anyone. So I will let them see my anger. I will destroy them with an anger that is like fire. This is because of all the things they have done, says the Lord God (Ezekiel 22:30–31).

Prayer a Divine Mystery

Have you thought about the design of prayer? Have you considered the plan God had in His mind regarding this great mystery? Why should there be such a thing as prayer? Surely God does not need it for Himself, for He is all-powerful. Does He need anything from man? God made the world, and everything else, and He keeps it in running condition. Should such a One need anything from us little humans? Why does so much depend on prayer? Why does Almighty God wait to hear a human pray before He works in the world of men? Why should He watch to see a man or woman cooperate through faith and prayer before He takes action? Why did God limit Himself in such a way? God has done many wonderful things by simply speaking a word. Then why does He waste time waiting for men and women to find time to pray?

God "Helpless" Without a Man

The mystery of the design of prayer is pointed out in Ezekiel 22:30–31. During a time when the nation of Israel pushed God out of their lives, God said, "I looked for someone to build up the walls. I looked for someone to stand before me where the walls are broken to defend these people. Then I would not have to destroy them. But I did not find anyone. So I will let them see my anger. I will destroy them with an anger that is like fire. This is because of all the things they have done, says the Lord God."

Here we gain understanding about our God and it is a wonder and a comfort. Beyond the wonder and comfort we see it is a high calling of great purpose. God is looking for a way, a means by which He will not need to exercise judgment. He longs to set the nation free from judgment. He does not want to punish them. Strange as it may seem, He cannot do this without help from one or more of the people of the earth. Without a praying one, judgment is sure to come. Why should God have to depend on those praying ones when He Himself wants to drop the whole idea of judgment? God is the almighty ruler of all the worlds. There is no one above Him. He does not have to ask a permit from anyone. Why does He not simply do His own will whether people pray or not? Why did He set up a system which makes Him depend on someone so weak as a human being? What a mystery this is!

God Begs Men to Pray

God made His plan to save the human race from terrible judgment by sending His Son Jesus Christ to the earth. After that, God waits for man to cooperate with Him so that His plan will not be wasted. It is a sad and bitter thought, but such a loss is possible. How shall we escape such waste and loss? In the Word of God He invites us to pray. He not only invites, but He begs us to pray. One way to express Matthew 7:7 is: "Ask, I ask you to ask; seek, I intreat you to seek; knock, I urge you to knock." It seems clear that He does nothing without our prayers.

God even commands us to pray. "Ask the Lord of the harvest, therefore, to send out workers into his harvest field" (Matthew 9:38, *NIV*). He is Himself the Lord of the harvest. The harvest is His. The laborers are His. Why should He stand "helplessly" by while He begs men to pray workers into the field? Why does He send workers only in answer to prayers?

God Promises to Answer, No Doubt About It

Again God shows us how important this design of prayer is. God clearly tells He will Himself answer our prayers. His invitation to pray and His promise to pay attention to the prayers is far reaching and includes anything and everything we might want. It is as if God offers us His rod and says, "You use it." Here are some examples: "And if you ask for anything in my name, I will do it for you. Then the Father's glory will be shown through the Son. If you ask me for anything in my name I will do it" (John 14:13–14). "Remain in me and follow my teachings. If you do this, then you can ask for anything you want, and it will be given to you" (John 15:7). "I tell you the truth. My Father will give you anything you ask for in my name. Until now you have not asked for anything in my name. Ask and you will receive. And your joy will be the fullest joy" (John 16:23–24).

His Plan of Prayer Is Safe and Sure

The promises God makes are without difficult and impossible conditions. That is, they ask only what is fair, what is possible for a child of God to keep or do. We are told to continue living in Jesus, exercising prayer and faith. This is quite possible for a person who has the Holy One living within. God has not made a set of conditions so hard that we cannot possibly obey them. That would not be fair, and God is fair in all His ways. It is up to us to pray, and to pray properly. It is our duty, and can become our great joy. God has done His part. Now it is up to us.

Yes, our prayers are conditioned by His will. This is really not a problem because we, His children, have the same desires that He has. His will is our will. So His plan of prayer is safe and sure. We do well to learn to exercise prayer and to exercise it often.

God Makes the Plans — His Church Carries Them Out

The offer God made (to share His ruling power) is a true offer that we can depend on. God did not make that offer without thought. He carefully planned it. When God designed prayer He was really inviting His Church to cooperate with Him in ruling. God Himself makes the decisions, but the men and women of God carry out those decisions. The work of carrying out His plans is placed on the shoulders of His Church. "So I tell you, you are Peter. And I will build my church on this rock. The power of death, the gates of hell, will not be able to defeat my church.[1] I will give you the keys of the kingdom of heaven. The things you don't allow on earth will be the things that God does not allow. The things you allow on earth will be the things that God allows" (Matthew 16:18–19). This promise is repeated to the whole Church in Matthew 18:18: "I tell you the truth. The things you don't allow on earth will be the things God does not allow. The things you allow on earth will be the things that God allows." "Listen! I gave *you* power, authority, to walk on snakes and scorpions. I gave you more power than the enemy has. Nothing will hurt you" (Luke 10:19). "As my Father sent me, I now send you. . . . If you forgive anyone his sins, they are forgiven. If you don't forgive them, they are not forgiven" (John 20:21–23).

God Makes Us His Deputies

Dr. Wilbur T. Dayton spoke on John 20:21–23 as part of the Easter Sunday School lesson for April 14, 1968. He said, "When Jesus returned to heaven in His human body, He left His disciples behind as His deputies. They were to take His place. They and we have a high calling. We are His deputies with power to act in His Name." "As my Father sent me, I now send you" can mean nothing less than that we are His deputies. We can see to it that His will is done on earth. This is only possible because He has given us His own authority.

Why?

The question is, *Why* did God choose to work within this system of prayer? *Why* did He place so much weight on the shoulders of weak, fallen men? *How* could He dare leave so much up to them? *Why* is it so important that His Church cooperate with Him in ruling the world? We do not accept the Roman idea that the Pope is the one and only deputy that God has on the earth. However, we may have forgotten one important thing. We may have forgotten that we are *all* deputies, able to exercise His power and see His kingdom spread over our part of the earth. How does man operate this power? Through *prayer* (Ezekiel 22:30–31). How can we explain this? Why did God do it?

Prayer — Our Opportunity and the Mark of Rank

God had something very great in mind when He planned the system of prayer. God had one single purpose when He made the worlds and the human race. God wanted a Bride, a Wife for His Son. This fact is part of the mystery that is seen in the book of Ephesians, and especially in the fifth chapter. There, in chapter five, it builds up until we come to a clear understanding, and get light on the whole matter. This chapter throws light on the human and divine marriage plans. The one is like the other. Verse 32 makes this very clear when it says that the marriage pair is Christ and the Church.[2] In the design and purpose of God, from the beginning, the Church is to fill the highest position there is after the position God Himself holds. As the Bride of the Son she will share with Him a place of ruling. "Surely you know that God's people will judge the world. . . . You know that in the future we will judge angels. So surely we can judge things in this life" (1 Corinthians 6:2–3). "If we accept suffering, then we will also rule with him" (2 Timothy 2:12). "I will give power to everyone who wins the victory and continues to the end to do what I want. I will give him power over the nations" (Revelation 2:26). "He who wins the victory will sit with me on my throne. It was the same with me. I won the victory and sat down with my Father on his throne" (Revelation 3:21). "And they all sang a new song to the Lamb: You are worthy to take the scroll and to open its seals, because you were killed; and with the blood of your death you bought men for God from every tribe, language, people, and nation. You made them to be a kingdom of priests for our God. And they will rule on the earth" (Revelation 5:9–10).

Saved members of the human race, the only race that was made in the image of God, will form this company called the Bride. Since this Bride is to share the throne (the place of ruling) with her Lover and Lord, she must be trained and prepared for this high position. It is the position of a queen.

Prayer Is On-the-job Training for Ruling

Now, at last, we are coming to the answer of the question we have been repeating, "Why did God dare leave so much up to the Church?" It is because of the high position the Church is later to fill. She must now have training. As the Church battles in her prayer closet, carrying out the will of God, she is being trained for a higher place. She is being trained to govern for future days, and those days without an end. This must all be done before the Marriage Supper of the Lamb. So that the Church could learn the great art of overcoming, God designed prayer.

Friends, this is the answer we have been working up to. God gives the Church on-the-job training by letting her carry out His will through prayer right here on earth. In this way she will develop the character needed for her position in the future heaven. God has made the Church able, yes, even now, to act in His place, to act for Him.

Notice how often *earth* as her place of action is spoken of: "The things you don't allow on *earth* . . . the things you allow on *earth*"; "Also, I tell you, that if two of you on *earth* agree about something . . ." (Matthew 16:19; Matthew 18:18–19). This act of God, giving the Christians such a place of ruling in earthly affairs, is the highest honor possible. It gives her the highest rank of all beings that God has made. Not even the angels will have such a rank. They were not made in the image of God. They were not made to be the Bride of Christ.

Highest Rank — The Original Purpose of God

Can it be possible? Yes, it is really true. God cannot raise man to a higher place and still keep His own place, high above all. Of course, the One who made all things is always above the ones He made. Yet, from the beginning God planned that there should be such a union that God and man would be of the same family. Man would have a part in the ruling of all the worlds. Jesus says, "He who wins the victory will sit with me on my throne. It was the same with me. I won the victory and sat down with my Father on his throne" (Revelation 3:21). This was no afterthought. It was the plan of God from the beginning. *"In Christ* he chose us before the world was made" (Ephesians 1:4). This was the original purpose of God when He decided to make man. The prayer idea was His plan to prepare or train the Bride for her high position.

If the Church Will Not Pray, God Will Not Act

God will not pass over His Church and do for her the things He gave her to do. He will not take things out of her hands. That would spoil His training plan. There is no other way for her to grow up into the character that is needed for her high position. This is why when she fails He will wait. When it comes to saving people from their sins, God waits for the Church to use her mighty weapons of prayer. If the Church will not pray God will not act because this would spoil His purpose. He purposes to train her through prayer. She would not fit into the position He has for her if she did not have the training.

This was the plan of God from the beginning. He will not spoil it now by taking things out of her hands. He will let the whole world destroy itself before He would take things out of her hands. God has done His part of the work and it is full and complete. He will not now override His Church. His purpose from the beginning was to get the Bride ready for His Son. God wants her to be ready for the governing process. This is only possible by active prayer. In this way she learns to enter into His purposes, pure and powerful as they are. For this reason *God will do nothing without His Church.*

Prayer — The Main Business of the Church

This is why John Wesley said, "God will do nothing but in answer to prayer." This is why S. D. Gordon said that "The greatest thing anyone can do for God and for man is to pray." This is why he also said, "You can do more than pray after you have prayed, but you cannot do more than pray *until* you have prayed." This also explains why he said, "Prayer is striking the winning blow — serving is gathering up the results." This explains why E. M. Bounds said, "God shapes the world through prayer. The more praying there is in the world the better the world will be, the stronger the forces against evil will be. . . . The prayers of the saints of God are like riches stored up in heaven. By these riches God does His work on earth. God conditions the very life of His cause on prayer." If these things are true, then "prayer should be the main business of our day."

The Church Holds the Key

Checks used by some business places require that two people sign them. If only one person signs such checks they will not be honored. Both parties must sign them. This teaches us the method God uses as He operates through the prayer and faith of His people. His promises are like checks signed in His blood. His part was finished at Calvary. Now it is up to us to sign that check too. We go into the closet of prayer and write our name down beside the name of God. We do this through prayer and faith. When that is done the riches are ours for the taking.

It is also like a safe box in a bank. The banker has a key and you have a key. Both keys must be used before you can have the money that is stored there for you. Heaven holds the key by which decisions governing earthly affairs are made. We hold the key by which those decisions are put into action.

As we understand this, prayer takes on new meaning for us. Prayer is not overcoming something in God, to break down His will, to force Him to do our will. It is binding upon earth that which has *already been bound* in heaven (Matthew 16:19, *AMP*). It is carrying out His decision. It is making His will come to pass on earth. Prayer makes it possible for the will of God to be done; He will not do it without our prayer. True prayer originates in the heart of God. It is He who puts the desire in our hearts and He has already planned the answer before we speak our prayer. When we understand this it is easier to have faith.

Too Busy to Pray

The angels have not been invited into the prayer life. The throne room is prepared not for the angels but for humans. Are we too busy to pray? Too busy watching TV? Listening to the sports? Hunting and fishing? Swimming and boating? Farming? Taking care of our business? Are we so busy with the cares and pleasures of life that we have no time to pray?

Maybe some are thinking: Are we to have nothing at

all for ourselves? The answer is NO. Christ is to be ALL and in all. You are not your own. You are bought with a price (1 Corinthians 6:19–20). "So if you eat, or if you drink, or if you do anything, do everything for the glory of God" (1 Corinthians 10:31). If you can buy the new car, the new home, the new furniture, work two jobs, etc., for the glory of God — well and good. But maybe your life-style is such that it takes too much time. Are we loving other things, work and play, so much that we have no time to pray? We are not only doing God a wrong, but our neighbor and ourselves also. When we fail to pray are we not spoiling the very plans God has made? We are robbing the world of that best plan God has made for it. We are also limiting our rank in the long life that waits for us after death. "I LOOKED FOR SOMEONE AMONG THEM BUT I DID NOT FIND ANYONE."

NOTES

1. Two Greek words used in this verse are much alike and yet different. One is *petros,* which happens to be Peter's name in Greek; the other is *petra*. Both *petros* and *petra* mean "rock." *Petra* means a very large rock, not able to be dug out of the ground; but *petros* means a rock by itself, dug out of the ground. Jesus is saying that He will build His Church, not on the small rock, dug out and alone, but on the very large rock, firm and fixed, on *petra* — that is, on Himself.

Jesus goes on to say that hell itself will not be able to do away with His Church. In the East, at that time, the seat of a city government was at the gate of the city. Plans and decisions were made at that place. Jesus is saying that all the plans that hell makes will not be able to destroy His Church.

If a person takes only a short, quick look around he might well say that the devil is the winner. If only numbers were considered, yes, we would say the devil would be the winner. However, we must look at the purpose of God. He is calling out and training a group of people to rule with Him. This is going on and Satan cannot stop it. Through the ages this has been true. The Church has passed through suffering, fire, dangers, hunger — troubles of all kinds. Instead of destroying the Church these things have further trained the Church. The gates of hell have not destroyed the Church.

2. The mystery of the heavenly marriage program is interesting because of the thought of the Bride being not one person but many. This is very different from the marriages we know. Paul helps us

understand this idea when he explains that the Church is a body. Many people make up this one body, that is, the Bride. "A person's body is only one thing, but it has many parts. Yes, there are many parts to a body, but all those parts make only one body. Christ is like that too. . . . And a person's body has more than one part. It has many parts" (1 Corinthians 12:12,14).

We consider the human body as a single person because it has one center for controlling thought. Yet Paul teaches that it has many members, not only one. Just so, the Holy City that John saw, which is the heavenly Bride, was not merely one person but a great company. Yet, because it will be united by one controlling center, it can be compared to the human body and its many parts.

The Church is moving towards this unity, working together as the parts of the human body work together. There will come a day when the oneness will be complete, and there will be perfect harmony, as John saw when he watched the Bride coming down out of heaven. This company of people will be perfectly joined because of their great love for the Bridegroom. They will be like one person. God considers unity among His people very, very important. It is a thing that Satan fights.

4

AUTHORITY: IT IS A GIFT FROM GOD

Listen! I gave you power to walk on snakes and scorpions. I gave you more power than the enemy has. Nothing will hurt you (Luke 10:19).

The Authority Given to the Church

In the Scriptures we read that Jesus sent out seventy disciples to go and preach the gospel and heal the sick. They returned with joy such as they had never experienced before. They reported on their success. The disciples were surprised to hear what Jesus had to say about their experiences. He said He had seen it happening! He had seen Satan being thrown out of his high place. It was His own word that had caused so many things to happen (Luke 10:18). Now He places in their hands that same word of authority. Now He is saying, "I hand this authority over to you." "I gave you power to walk on snakes and scorpions. I gave you more power than the enemy has. Nothing will hurt you" (Luke 10:19).

This statement gives the Church her authority, her right to command in the battle with Satan. This authority also sets the Church free from any hold of Satan. It gives us the right to do battle with Satan. It is clear from this and other verses in Scripture what God plans for the Church. *It is the Church and not Satan that is to be the controlling influence in the world.*

Union

Read Ephesians 1:20–22. We find here that Christ is the final authority. He has been lifted up above every name or power. All authority in both heaven and earth has been put under His feet. Paul adds that Jesus is also the Head of the Church. The Church is His body. This is a union as to purpose or use, but it goes even further. Our life itself is joined with His. There is a joining together that is even closer than the joining of a man to a woman in marriage.

The Union Expressed by Pictures

God made a bride for Adam. This was like a shadow or picture pointing to the coming union of Christ and His Church. When God made all the animals — so different and so wonderful — He looked them over. Not a one was fit company for Adam. They did not share his nature. So Adam was sent into a "deep sleep." From a wound in his side, God took a bone and formed a woman. She was a fit helper for Adam. "Now there was a being in life who could understand Adam. She could enter into his plans, hopes and fears. She could love as he loved. She could live as Adam lived. The animals that God had created could not do this" (T. H. Nelson). "And the man said, Now, this is someone whose bones came from my bones. Her body came from my body" (Genesis 2:23). This was a meeting of two beings who were alike in nature.

In 1 Corinthians 15:44–47 Christ is called "the second man" or the "last Adam." Adam had a bride. Christ also must have a bride. Like the first Adam it was necessary that Christ also experience a "deep sleep." His was a sleep of death and rising again. Out of His wounded side the Church, through faith, is born of God. She is born the Bride of Christ. In Revelation 21:9 she is called the Bride, the Wife of the Lamb. Paul speaks of this in chapter five of Ephesians. In verse 30 he says that as Eve was taken from Adam, so "we are parts of his body." The Church is His body now. She will be His Bride at the Marriage Supper of the Lamb.

On the Throne Because of This Real, Living Union

From all that has been said we realize that the union with Jesus Christ is a very real thing. We know also that Christ has been given the highest place of authority and command. Since the Church is joined to Jesus, where does that put the Church? Where else can she be but on the throne with Jesus Christ? This agrees with Paul as he writes in Ephesians 2:5–6. He says that we were made alive with Christ. He says that God raised us up with Jesus and made us sit in heavenly places in Christ Jesus.

This means that we are truly with Christ on His throne. We have already begun to rule with Christ. We were with Christ in His death, in His rising again, in His being lifted up, and now we are seated with Him.[1]

The Practical Effects of This Union

To the natural mind this seems foolish, yet it is true. In spite of her weaknesses, her failings, her mistakes and her sins, there is no force in the world as powerful as the Church of Jesus Christ. One civilization after another has been destroyed because of their turning away from God and His truth. "People on earth did what God said was evil. Violence was everywhere. And God saw this evil. All people on the earth did only evil. So God said to Noah, 'People have made the earth full of violence. So I will destroy all people from the earth'" (Genesis 6:11–13).

It is the same today. Satan would like total rule in human affairs. There is only one force in the world that can stop him from having that. That force is the Church of the living God. If Satan were given free run of things, beauty and goodness would be no more. Satan would make a hell of life right here and now.

All the saving and healing virtue that we know in our sad world flows from the cross of Calvary. The actions of men are all selfish unless they have their origin in the very life of Jesus. He it is who gave His blood for us. His was a life totally lived for others. It had no selfish stream. Were this not so there would be no goodness in this world. Total selfishness means total hate. And that means hell.

Civilization a By-product of the Gospel

In a limited way we experience a certain peace and quietness in life. Without this there could be no social order or civilization as we know it. This peace and quietness is caused by the gospel, and the true Church is the caretaker of the gospel. It is the base of society and government. Without the moral and spiritual light brought by the Word of God, business, politics, education and society in general would find great difficulty in operating. Government cannot function without order. Reverence for God brings order to a country. Civilization as we know it, with a high standard of living, is surely a by-product of the gospel.

The Church Controls the Balance of Power

From the Bible, then, are born all the character qualities that make up the foundation of our moral, spiritual, social and political well-being. The Church is in charge of that truth. So far as the Church has been faithful to that trust she has spiritually influenced the affairs of men. So far as she has been faithful she has had a good effect in our world. So far as she has been faithful to her trust she has delayed the day of total judgment.

Jesus was not speaking empty words when He said to His disciples in Matthew 5:13,14: "You are the salt of the earth"; "You are the light that gives light to the world." The world at large is blind to this fact. Yet, if it were not for the pure and clean power of the Christian Church, civilization as we know it would soon disappear. So we see that the Church has a keeping power. *Therefore, by virtue of her union with Jesus Christ, the Church, not Satan, holds the balance of power in human affairs.*

It has been truly said, *"The fate of the world is in the hands of nameless saints."* This truth is wonderfully expressed in Psalm 149:5–9: "Let those who worship him rejoice in his glory. Let them sing for joy even in bed! Let them shout his praise with their two-edged swords in their hands. They will punish the nations. They will defeat the people. They will put those kings in chains and those important men in iron bands. They will punish them as God has written."

If it were not for the Church Satan would already have turned this world into a hell. The fact that the world still exists proves this: At least a part of the Church is already living in union with her Lord. She is already busy with her on-the-job training for her future position — ruling with Christ.

George Washington, the first President of the United States of America, recognized these truths when he said, "It is impossible to rightly govern the world without God and the Bible." And that prince of a man, Daniel Webster, said, "If we abide by the teachings of the Bible our country will go on from blessing to blessing; but if we or our children forget its teachings and its authority, no man can tell how suddenly we may be destroyed and all our glory will be forgotten." In the light of present conditions these words sound a warning for us.

The Authority of the Church and Free Will[2]

These truths are fairly well recognized, as far as world affairs are considered. Do these truths also hold good in our personal lives? Consider a person who is not yet saved. Who holds the power of influence over that unsaved person, Satan or the Church? Does the authority which Christ has offered the Church also affect the choice of a free moral being?[3] What does this authority have to do with free moral choice? God has said in His Word that He wills that men be saved. Knowing this, can the Church pray for any person who is not saved with the full faith that he will be saved? Or must the one who prays remember that even God will not force a person to come to Him against his will? Must we say, as we often do, that because "so and so" has free moral choice, all we can do is pray and leave the rest to God?

We know that when we pray for a person to be saved we are praying according to the will of God. In 1 John 5:14–15 we read, "We can come to God with no doubts. This means that when we ask God for things (and those things agree with what God wants for us), then God cares about what we say. God listens to us every time we ask him. So we know that he gives us the things that we ask from him." Now the question is: Can the free moral choice of man destroy the power of this promise? Do we have to stand back and watch Satan demand a soul as his own because God does not cross the will of a single person? Is it true to say that all we can do is pray and leave the rest to God and the person prayed for? These are weighty matters, and we must look into them carefully.

Were We Not All Enemies of God?

May I answer this question by asking another? *Do you believe that anyone was saved who was not at first an enemy of God?* Were we not all born with our backs to God? Did we not all, like Adam, run and hide from God? Did we not all fight against God when He was trying to win us to Himself? Finally it became more painful to fight than to yield to God. At that point we quit running and listened to God.

The One Special Factor that Settles the Matter of Being Saved

Is this not the general path of the journey from being an enemy of God to becoming His friend? Jesus says, "No one can come to me unless the Father draws him to me" (John 6:44). And the Father always draws by means of the Spirit. We know that God does not respect one person above another. We also know that He wants all men to be saved, and that He seeks all men (John 1:9). Since this is the case, why is God successful in His seeking some and not others? Might this be the answer to that question: For some there has been strong prayer offered up to God. Wesley said, "God does nothing but in answer to prayer." Does this make matters clear? Some praying people have not been willing that Satan should have their loved one. They have prayed with strong prayer and tears. To this they added a word of command.

God has provided salvation for all people. "Look, the Lamb of God. He takes away the sins of *the world!*" (John 1:29). "Jesus is the way our sins are taken away. And Jesus is the way that *all people* can have their sins taken away, too" (1 John 2:2). God wants all men to be saved and He has provided for that. *Strong prayer that cares and commands makes a difference.* Because of it souls are saved. All others are in the greatest danger. "After he said this, he breathed on them and said, 'Receive the Holy Spirit. If you forgive anyone his sins, they are forgiven; if you don't forgive them, they are not forgiven'" (John 20:22–23).[4]

The Spirit and the Bride

The Holy Spirit has the power to give light to the mind and to wake up the spirit. He can move on the heart of a man so that man will find it easier to yield to God than to continue as an enemy of God. *Yet God will not work alone, without man. If man will not do his part in praying, God will wait.* God has chosen to train His followers so that they will be prepared to rule with Him. This training includes learning to care like Jesus cares. That kind of caring will change our style of praying. "The Spirit *and the Bride* say, Come" (Revelation 22:17). Not the Spirit alone, but the Spirit *and* the Bride. *He will do nothing without her.*[5]

If the Church does not do strong praying, the Spirit does not court. If the Spirit does not seek or court, the soul is lost. But the Spirit will seek every soul of whom the Church declares, "This one belongs to God."

The Power of Life and Death

And so we see the power of the Church. Not only does the Church hold the balance of power in world affairs, but also in the matter of the salvation of souls. *She holds the power of life and death over the souls of men.* God does not force a person against his will. The Holy Spirit is, of course, very good at making people change their minds. But He wants His children to cooperate with Him in this matter. They cooperate chiefly by their prayer. We believe this explains, at least in part, why some are saved and others are lost.

The Damascus Road Experience

We will consider Paul and his experience of salvation. Paul was an enemy of the early Church. The Bible does not tell us that the Church was praying for Paul, but we may be sure that they did. The life of the Church was in danger because of Paul. They had good reason to pray for him! Knowing that God so reached and won the heart of Paul, we should not give up. Praying works wonders.

The Mighty Weapons that Paul Used

Possibly you still have problems about the free will of man. Because God made man with a free will, you perhaps doubt the power of the Church. Do you still feel we should simply pray but must leave the result to that certain person? Listen to Paul as he speaks in 2 Corinthians 10:4–5: "I use God's mighty weapons, not those made by man, to knock down the devil's strongholds. These weapons can break down every proud argument against God and every wall that can be built to keep men from finding him. *With these weapons I can capture rebels and bring them back to God, and change them into men whose heart's desire is obedience to Christ*" (LB).

Freedom of Choice

When Paul wrote those words did he overlook the free moral choice of man? Or was Paul thinking about his own experience on the road to Damascus? Was he remembering what that Voice from heaven was saying to him about kicking against Him? Was he thinking about how his own heart was changed that day? Was he not perhaps thinking that the weapons used to win him (Paul) could also be used to win others?

Notice that using these weapons does not mean that man no longer has a choice. God does not use force. By using these weapons He causes the sinner to cooperate of his own accord. He becomes a willing servant of Christ. If Paul could use weapons such as these, can we not also use them?

An Enemy Won Over

My mother used these weapons on me. I was as much against God as any sinner. I was fighting with all my might. But the time came when it was easier for me to lay down my weapons than to continue to fight. The way the Holy Spirit pressed me became so powerful that I had to give up. I finally *wanted* to give up. I fell into the arms of my God, glad the fight was over.

When the Church learns to use her weapons, God deals with the sinner. It is my belief that if a soul has not crossed over that serious place from which there is no returning, a believing Church may pray him into salvation. Hallelujah!

"FOR AS SOON AS ZION TRAVAILED, SHE BROUGHT FORTH HER CHILDREN" (Isaiah 66:8, *KJV*).

NOTES

1.   Many people have problems with this teaching of union with Christ. How can we be seated in heavenly places when our feet touch earth every day? Paul gives us the key to this mystery in 1 Corinthians 6:17: "But the one who joins himself with the Lord is one with the Lord in spirit." The spirit is more important and more lasting than the body. Consider this: when a man dies, his body soon turns to dust. That is, without a spirit (for it has gone away in death) the body has little value. The body depends on the spirit and is no good without it. The spirit never dies; it is real in itself. Your spirit is the real you, the real person. *Therefore, a person who is joined to the Lord as one spirit is, in his true being, seated with Christ in the heavens.* Even while the body is here, the real self is with Christ on the throne. And because "the one who joins himself with the Lord is one with the Lord in spirit," where He *is,* there we *will be.* That includes a place on the throne.

2.   In all that we have written or will write, we want to make one point very clear: If a person is not saved he can blame no one but himself. The Church's duty ends with faithfulness in praying for the sinner. Only the Holy Spirit knows when this point is reached. The lost sinner cannot point at someone else and say, "It's all your fault." The choice still lies with him.

3.   The words "a free moral being" are not used here in the total or

complete sense. Only God is a free moral being in the complete sense. Because of the fall of man, man is no longer as he once was. Each man must give an answer to God for his actions.

4. There have been differences of opinion about the meaning of John 20:23: "If you forgive anyone his sins, they are forgiven. If you don't forgive them, they are not forgiven." It almost shocks us that Christ has given such authority (the power to forgive sins) to the Church. However, in a real sense, it is true. The Church exercises the authority God has given her. She uses her tools, prayer and faith. By so doing she opens the way for the Holy Spirit to do His work — courting, leading, influencing. All this causes the sinner to be set free from the forces that hold him. In this condition he is more able to make a good choice. God, of course, is the one who does the forgiving. Because of her praying, the Church is cooperating with God in the work of forgiving. In that sense she has the authority to forgive. This authority cannot be limited to a priest or minister, for according to the New Testament every believer is a priest.

5. In the Old Testament, Israel was considered as the wife of Jehovah. In the New Testament the Church has taken the place of Israel, so we could say the Church is like the wife of our Lord. "In the same way, my brothers, your old selves died, and you became free from the law through the body of Christ. Now you belong to someone else. You belong to the One who was raised from death. We belong to Christ so we can be used in service to God" (Romans 7:4).

In the earthly human family, it takes two to bring new life into being, the husband and the wife. In a like way, a spiritual child is not born without the agreement and cooperation of the Father (God) and the mother (Church). And a child is not born without suffering. It is not easy to bring a child into the world. Neither is it easy to bring a soul from darkness to light, that is, to bring about a spiritual birth. The Church and the Spirit are both necessary. "The Spirit *and* the Bride say, come."

5

THE LAWS THAT GIVE THE CHURCH HER AUTHORITY

Was Calvary a Victory or a Loss?

It is very important for every believer to know the answer to this question. Calvary (the place where Jesus died) was a victory so great that it is impossible to overstate it. It is very important that believers understand this. They must also believe it beyond all doubt. Failing in this, the believer will not be able to exercise his authority over Satan. This chapter and the next are written to help Christians be free of all doubt in this matter. Paul speaks of Satan and his forces as "the dethroned powers that rule" (1 Corinthians 2:6, *Moffatt*).

Satan also has a church, called by that name. That church teaches that Calvary was a big mistake, a foolish thing without meaning or strength.

The church of Satan has as their base *The Satanic Bible*. In it they describe the cross with our Lord on it as "a washed-out nobody hanging on a tree." Satan is shown as taking authority away from Christ. Christ is described as "the king without power," "running away and unable to speak," and many other dirty names to bring His honor down to shame. Satan is described as "Great Satan," "Prince of Darkness," "Satan — Lucifer who rules the earth," and even "Lord of light."

Satan always seeks to prove to the world and to the Church that he is almost, if not quite, as powerful as God. The world, for the most part, believes his lies. The Church suffers from them. The Church suffers because Satan has managed to hide from the Church what really happened to him. To the world at large, and to some believers too, the death on the cross seems to be a terrible mistake, a losing, not a winnng. Even though we say that we believe, many of us have a nervous fear that, after all, Satan had the victory at Calvary. As we study we will see that, beyond a doubt, the Lord Jesus won the victory.

The Mission Given to Adam: Controlling the Earth

Before we can understand what happened at Calvary, we need to understand what happened when Adam fell into sin. We speak from the view of the law. Man was originally made for authority. God shaped man for that. When Adam was first made, God put him in charge of the whole world and all that was in the world. In Genesis 1:26 it says, "Then God said, let us make human beings in our image, and likeness; and let them rule over the fish in the sea and the birds in the sky. Let them rule over the tame animals, over all the earth, and over all the small crawling animals on the earth." The writer of the eighth psalm adds this word: "You put him in charge of everything you made. You put all things under his control."

The Failure of Adam and the Wreck That Resulted

The whole world and the heavens around it are governed by law. The buying back of the human race is also based on a system of godly laws, just and pure. When God gave man the right to rule the earth, it was a real and true gift. It belonged to him by right of law. It was up to Adam what he would do with this authority. God does not give and then take back His gifts. That would go against His own laws of right and wrong. It would have been without due process of law.

Looking For a Match and More Than a Match for the Enemy

When Adam chose to obey Satan, Satan became his master. "Surely you know that when you give yourselves like slaves to obey someone, then you are really slaves of that person" (Romans 6:16). As a servant of Satan, Adam lost his right to himself and to the world he was to rule. Adam yielded those rights to Satan. That is the price Adam paid.

How could this be changed? How could Adam once more have the right to rule? God is not like the world rulers of today who simply take authority, right or not. God had His angels (heaven, I suppose, is full of them) and they are mighty. However, they were not made to handle this problem. The angels had never been given the right to rule the world. This was not their business; they were not made for such work. If Adam and his race were to be saved, it had to be done by a human being.

The government of the earth had been given to man. It was lost by man — it could only be saved by a man. But what man was fit to do such mighty work? Adam and all his race had become servants of Satan, so they were not fit deliverers. Adam and his race were not only servants, they were slaves. A slave has no right when it comes to the law. So we see that a member of the human race had to be found who was not a slave of Satan.

The Problem Taken Care Of: The Birth of Jesus

To the human mind the case was hopeless, but *God found a way*. "But when the right time came, God sent his Son. His Son was born of a woman and lived under the law. God did this so that he could buy freedom for those who were under the law. His purpose was to make us his children" (Galatians 4:4–5). *God found the cure for the problem by the birth of His own Son*. Because of the Holy Spirit, the godly nature was found in Jesus Christ. There was no sin in Jesus. Therefore, as Jesus Himself said, "He [Satan] has no power over me." In no way could Satan control Jesus. Because "he was born of a woman" He was a true human being. He belonged to the human race. Jesus Christ, by right of law, could enter the fight to set man free.

It Was Necessary That Jesus Be Born Without a Human Father

Jesus was a human but He was also the Son of God.

He was not just a human being. He was more. Some people say that it makes no difference whether Jesus had a human father or not. They are wrong! To enter the battle with Satan, Jesus had to have both the godly and the human nature (Luke 1:35).

It Was Necessary to Be Perfect

· Yes, it was necessary for Jesus to be one of the human race to enter the battle, but that was not all. He needed to be one who was pure and without sin, even when tried. If there were sin in His life, Jesus also would have come under the control of Satan. To be fit as far as the law is concerned, Jesus had to be a true human person. To be fit as far as morals go, Jesus had to be perfect, that is, have a godly nature.

Jesus, as a Man, in Battle with Satan

As far as the law goes, Satan had no right to Jesus Christ. Satan tried to get control of Jesus by finding fault with His moral character. Satan tried to break the union that Jesus had with His Father. If Satan could cause Jesus to act on His own, apart from His Father, Satan would have won the battle. This was his master plan. This was the heart of the struggle between Jesus and Satan. *The whole future of the world and the human race hung on the way this struggle would turn out.* Satan did all he could. If he could make Jesus think even one thought apart or different from that of the heavenly Father, Satan would have won. He would then have been the ruler of the world and of the human race. With the first Adam Satan had been the winner. And with the second Adam?

Although Jesus was "very God of very God," He had

to fight this battle and win as "very man of very man." The second Adam (Jesus) used the same weapons that had been given to the first Adam. If Jesus had used heavenly weapons, or better weapons than Adam had, the battle would not have been fair. *Jesus fought the battle as a man.*

The Struggle of the Ages

The battle went on from Jesus' birth to the cross. In order to regain what Adam lost, the Son of God was locked with Satan in battle. Through thirty-three years the battle continued in full force. Satan, before he fell, was called Lucifer. He had been the bringer of light guarding the throne of God. Of all the beings made before Adam, Lucifer was one of the highest in rank. Satan gathered all the powers from his dark world and joined them together in the fight. He tried to use them as a tool to break the connection between the heavenly Father and His Son. One slip on the part of Jesus and all would have been lost for the human race.

That cruel enemy tried to kill Jesus when He was a baby. Satan tried to make Jesus bow to him in the desert where He was tested. Satan worked through the religious people of that day. They turned many people against Jesus, tried several times to kill Him, and finally did just that. During all this time Satan watched for the breaking down of the union between Father and Son. Satan waited for Jesus to yield to him on even one small point — that would have been enough.

Tried in the Desert

Jesus was tried by Satan in the desert, alone, away

from other people. Satan offered Jesus a shortcut to world control. "Fall down and worship me" — just once. Satan said that the whole world was under his control and that he could give it to anyone he chose. He was quite willing to give it to Jesus for a single bending of His knee.

Jesus knew that the world was under the control of the evil one. This was according to law. Jesus also knew there was only one way to take control away from Satan. That way was the cross. Jesus won the battle in that desert place by using the Word of God. That same weapon (the Word of God) is given to us. We can win in the same way!

Gethsemane

The battle continued all through Jesus' earthly life, but the force of it greatly increased in Gethsemane (the place of prayer just before His death). Satan pressed against Jesus there in that garden with terrible force. Satan fought against His spirit until Jesus was at the very gate of death. Jesus cried, "My heart is full of sorrow and breaking with sadness" (Matthew 26:38). Drops of blood fell from His face to the ground, so deeply was Jesus troubled.

To Understand His Suffering

The thought of dying on a cross was not easy nor pleasant. Yet there were other thoughts more painful. The pain in His spirit was the worst thing. Jesus suffered the pain of a pure spirit being "made sin" (2 Corinthians 5:21). He took our sin on Him. That is to say, Jesus was so joined to our sin that His Father had to turn away. It was not just in words, it was real. He died as a sin offering. He was punished for our sins. He was judged as if He Himself had done all those sins. This was necessary to satisfy the demands of the law. Sin must be punished. Someone had to suffer the punishment, and as we have explained, no one else was fit to do it.

The battle in Gethsemane was, "Shall I refuse to drink this cup?" Jesus' soul was "exceeding sorrowful, even unto death" (*KJV*). The pain, too great for human words to express it properly, caused the drops of blood to roll down His face. "My Father, if it is possible, do not give me this cup of suffering. But do what you want, not what I want" (Matthew 26:39). Here it seems that the height of His suffering was reached. "But not what I want" — the future of the whole world rested on those words. With that decision the choice was made, the story was told. Jesus had accepted "the cup." After Gethsemane there was more quiet in His spirit although the pain in His body — the beating and the crown of thorns — grew worse by the minute. However, a little later, the suffering in His spirit again grew worse. When His Father hid His face (because of the load of sin) the suffering was the worst of all for Jesus. It broke His heart. He bowed His head and died.

Satan Beaten and Whipped

Satan pushed Jesus clear up to death. He had tried his best to make Jesus turn from God to him, that is, to Satan. Satan failed. Not once did Jesus turn away from His heavenly Father. Even at the moment of death, Jesus yielded His spirit into the care of the Father. Instead of anger or hate towards God, Jesus expressed only love and trust. Satan failed in his purpose. Jesus won, although He had to die in order to win.

When the results of Calvary are carefully considered, there is no question: *It is the victory of the ages!* When Jesus died without a touch of sin on His soul it was clear that Satan had no right to Jesus in any way. Besides this, it was also clear that Satan had lost his right to the human race! In general law, if a man kills another, he himself will be killed. So he that kills destroys himself. Now Satan had killed millions of people before he killed Jesus — he had caused the killings, that is. However, there was a difference. Until this time, by law, it was his right to kill. Satan was not a murderer, for the human race belonged to him. But now Satan had killed a man who was righteous, a man who was not his. For the first time, he became a murderer.[1] So in the courts of heaven *Satan was judged worthy of death*. This helps us understand the meaning of Hebrews 2:14: "These children are people with physical bodies. So Jesus himself became like them and had the same experiences they have. He did this so that, by dying, he could destroy the one who has the power of death." If this means anything, it means that Satan is now "destroyed" — ruined! According to law Satan has no more right nor part in the earth, nor in the people of the earth. He did have a big place before the cross, but he has that no longer.

A person under final sentence of death has no rights whatever. *Therefore, since Calvary, Satan has no rights upon anyone or anything*. Whatever authority Satan had before, it has now passed into the hands of the New Man (Christ Jesus). What Adam lost, Jesus Christ won back, but at what a price! Our Lord won the victory! Hallelujah!

NOTES

1. This does not go against John 8:44. We read in 1 John 3:15 that "Anyone who hates his brother is a murderer." In this sense Satan was a killer or murderer from the beginning. As far as the courts of law are concerned, however, Satan became a murderer only when he killed Jesus.

6

THE MIGHTY AND POWERFUL VICTORY OF CHRIST

Down Into Hell

The victory of Christ was completely just and right. This victory had in it a power and force beyond and above any power in this earth. The mighty force of that victory was such that no power in heaven or hell could overcome it. Because Jesus was "made sin" (2 Corinthians 5:21) He was charged through and through with our sins. He was covered inside and out with our sin. This is the reason that God could not look on Him. Jesus and sin were joined. They formed a union. In this condition Jesus could and did suffer for the sins of all men. He satisfied the demands of the law. He suffered as if He had sinned Himself, as if all the sin was His own personal crime and evil doing. His soul was made an offering for sin, for the sins of all people and of all time (Isaiah 53:10).

The sense of rightness would be destroyed if there were no accounting or dealing with sin. A holy sense of right and wrong demands that something be done about sin. Someone must deal with sin. It was not enough that Christ give up His physical life. That He did, but that alone was not enough. He also had to offer up His own pure human spirit (Ephesians 4:9 and Acts 2:27).[1] Sin is, after all, a thing of the spirit, and so we must deal with it in that way. Christ suffered on the cross in a physical way and a spiritual way. The pain in His body was physical. The separation from His Father was spiritual.

The heaviest punishment had to be paid. He must "taste death for every man" (Hebrews 2:9, *KJV*). Christ had to pay, once and for all, the price or punishment of sin. This means that He suffered what the whole human race together should have suffered. Then He went down into hell, the place of departed spirits. In hell Jesus declared His victory and brought out with Him a great company of followers. Hallelujah!

The Deep Pain of Making All Things Right and Good

Many people believe that the pain Jesus suffered in His spirit is described in Psalm 88: "You have brought me close to death. I am almost in the dark place of the dead. My life is full of troubles. I am nearly dead. I have been left as dead, like a body lying in a grave. You have been very angry with me. All your waves crush me. My eyes are weak from crying. Lord, I have prayed to you every day. I have lifted my hands in prayer to you. I have been weak and dying since I was young. I suffer from your terrors, and I am helpless. You have been angry with me. Your terrors have destroyed me" (Verses 6,3,5,7,9,15 and 16 in that order). We human people can never, never understand how deep His suffering was. His suffering is probably best described in the words of the prophet, "He poured out his soul unto death" (Isaiah 53:12, *KJV*). He suffered in our place until, in the mind of God, the law (demanding all things just and right) demanded no more. The law was satisfied. Isaiah 53:11: "He will suffer many things in his soul. But then he will see life and be satisfied."

The Pain of the Father

We wonder with great wonder as we consider the sufferings of Jesus the Son. Are we in danger of forgetting God the Father? "God [the Father] so loved the world that he gave his only begotten Son." Jesus was not the only one who suffered. It is impossible to understand what God the Father felt in His heart when He had to turn away from His only Son. The Father turned away from Jesus when He was covered with our sins. It was at this point that Jesus suffered the most. Something of the cost to God can be understood as we read Romans 8:32: "He that spared not his own Son, but delivered him up for us all, how shall he not with him also freely give us all things?" (*KJV*). Judgment against sin is no small matter. God, hating sin, had to turn Himself away from Jesus when He was covered with our sins. Sin cannot be forgotten or left alone. It has to be punished. Jesus suffered that punishment. Read Psalm 88 again.

Think again for a moment of the cost to the Father. The full force of His anger against sin (all the sin of all time) fell on His only Son. From this there was no escape for the Father. Centuries before, this was expressed by Isaiah, "Yet it was the Lord's good plan to bruise him and fill him with grief. But when his soul has been made an offering for sin, then he shall have a multitude of children, many heirs. He shall live again and God's program shall prosper in his hands. And when he [the Father] sees all that is accomplished by the anguish of his soul, he [the Father] shall be satisfied; and because of what he has experienced, my righteous Servant shall make many to be counted righteous before God, for he shall bear all their sins" (Isaiah 53:10-11, *LB*). This is the price the Father paid, a price no man can measure. God paid this price that He might have His own family, those born of His very own nature. And since Jesus offered Himself "through the eternal Spirit" (Hebrews 9:14), the Father, Son and Holy Spirit shared equally in the high cost of winning man back.

The Victory in the Lowest Hell

The law demands perfection. When that demand was satisfied Christ was "vindicated in the spirit" (1 Timothy 3:16, *NASB*). He then was "made alive in the spirit" (1 Peter 3:18, *NASB*). Jesus had been completely cut off and separated from God because of our sin. When He was perfected and made alive, declared right and perfect in the high courts of heaven, the tables were turned! The victory that Jesus won is described by Peter in Acts 2:24:

"God raised Jesus from death. God set him free from the pain of death. Death could not hold him." From this we understand that hell tried its very hardest, using every means that could be gathered to stop our Lord. Jesus, a real, true flesh-and-blood man, destroyed the power of Satan. Jesus left hell with the shout of victory. This place of the dead had never heard such a shout. Paul said that "God spoiled the spiritual rulers and powers," and "he showed the world that they were powerless" (Colossians 2:15). According to *Webster's New World Dictionary* this word "spoiled" means to "strip the hide from an animal," to "take away all arms or tools from the enemy who has already lost the battle." It also means "to damage or hurt in such a way as to make useless," to "destroy." This is what Jesus did to Satan after Jesus was made alive in the spirit. We get an idea of the greatness of the struggle when we read the words, "It was *not possible* that he should be held by it." Death wanted to keep hold of Jesus forever, not to let Him go. All the powers of the underworld joined their forces. They tried their best to prevent Jesus from rising from the dead. It was not possible. It was impossible for death to "keep its prey." In the words of the psalm writer, "He breaks down bronze gates. And he cuts apart iron bars" (Psalm 107:16). When Jesus left hell in great victory He took with Him the keys of death and hell. "I am the One who lives. I was dead, but look: I am alive forever and ever! And I hold the keys of death and where the dead are" (Revelation 1:18).

The great painter Michelangelo gave us a picture of this event, as he understood it. Michelangelo painted the doorway of that old prison, hell, and he showed the door torn off. Under it was pinned a demon, crushed beneath the fallen door. Truly, "death could not hold Him." An able writer has described the scene of victory. "Forcing a mighty earthquake, He mounted up again to solid earth, the light of day, and to the world of breathing men. Up and up again through the clouds and ranks of shouting angels, Jesus rose. He rose, the everlasting doors making room and opening up for Him. He continued to rise until He took His seat at the right hand of the Holy One on high. In the farthest heavens, in all the kingdoms of all the worlds, in the huge spaces of light or darkness, in all times, there is no one to equal our Lord Jesus. There is no power but that it owes everything to the Son of God. He is Lord over all. In the heavens there are ranks. Some are higher, some are lower. Jesus Christ stands clear above them all. Christ died on the cross and He rose from the grave in human form. Today He shares the throne with the Father. He is a human filled with all the fullness of God. Without any limits, He is Head over *all* things." Yes, today, a true human flesh-and-blood person shares the throne with the heavenly Father, exercising the power to govern. His name is Jesus.

Christ Was Lifted Up, and Also the Church

When Christ took His seat in heaven, He proved one thing: Satan was destroyed, undone. Hell was left in a terrible condition — no power. Satan was stripped of his power as far as the law is concerned. Besides that, Satan was stripped of his weapons. Yet there is more! When Jesus left the place of death all believers were also raised and seated together with Him. This is because of His great love for us. "But God's mercy is great, and he loved us very much. We were spiritually dead because of the things we did wrong against God. But God gave us new life with Christ. You have been saved by God's grace. And he raised us up with Christ and gave us a seat with him in the heavens. He did this for those of us who are in Christ Jesus" (Ephesians 2:4–6).

Joined with Christ in His Dying and Rising Again

In the mind of God every believer shares the life of Christ from the cross to the throne. According to the Word, we are crucified with Him, buried with Him, raised with Him, lifted up with Him and seated with Him (Romans 6 and Ephesians 2). How can this be? Consider the following:

All the sin of all the world could not be laid on Jesus except that the sinners also would be laid on Him. There is no such thing as sin apart from the sinner. When Jesus went to the cross He carried the entire human race with Him. "The love of Christ controls us. Because we know that One died for all. So all have died" (2 Corinthians 5:14). "I was put to death on the cross with Christ. I do not live anymore — it is Christ living in me. I still live in my body, but I live by faith in the Son of God. He loved me and gave himself to save me" (Galatians 2:20). "This teaching is true: If we died with him, then we will also live with him" (2 Timothy 2:11). Those who believe *share with Him* in His rising again and being seated in a governing place.

Joined With Christ in His High Place of Ruling

It does not surprise us that *He* should have that high

place of ruling. We know *He* is worthy. The hard part to believe is that *we* have been lifted up there with Him. Yet if "the one who joins himself with the Lord is one with the Lord in spirit" (1 Corinthians 6:17), it must be true.

We are not surprised that "all things have been put under *his* feet." However, we have failed to understand that as we are a part of Him, all things are also under *our* feet. That is our position in Christ. We have also failed to understand another thing. We do not realize that He is "the head over everything *for the church*" (Ephesians 1:22). *Christ has taken this place for the good of the Church.* Christ, as Head, directs the Church into all His purposes for her.

The Church is more important in the plan of God than we think. God has had His eye on the Church *from the very beginning.* She (the Church) is *the reason for all His action. God does nothing just for Himself. He always has the Church in mind.* The Church is His body, the fullness of Him that fills all things everywhere. He is not full or complete without His Church which is His body. God chose it to be this way.

In the truest sense, God needs no one. He is perfectly complete in Himself. However, God has chosen to limit Himself in order that the Church should be lifted up to union with Him. The Body cannot act without the Head. It is of no use without the Head. Just as true, the Head, by His own choice, cannot act without the Body. There must be a working together. *Without this working together the purposes of God will not come to pass.*

United With Christ in His Battle With Satan

This same truth is taught in the figure of the vine and

the branches. "Remain in me and I will remain in you. No branch can produce fruit alone" (John 15:4). The vine also needs the branches to bear the fruit. *God has limited Himself.* He cannot succeed in His purpose without the Church. Because God has limited Himself, the Body is as necessary as the Head, when it comes to action. The branch and the vine are *both* necessary. The Head and the Body also are *both* necessary. The Lord Jesus has limited Himself so that the Body might reach and experience everything that is possible for her to know in practical ways.

God has limited Himself *for a purpose.* He wants His followers (the Church) to be like His own Son. God wants to "bring many sons to glory." *God does not want His children to miss out on any good thing that is possible for them to experience.* He has taken us into His family as "His very own." He has taken us in as sons and daughters, born into His family. He does not consider us as simply something He had made. We are part "of the divine nature." When Christ took away the weapons of His enemy, we were there *with Him.* When Jesus picked up the keys to death and Hades (the place of the dead) and left in victory, we were *with Him.* When He took His place, seated with God, we were *with Him.* Satan and his angels are beneath the feet of Jesus. *They are beneath ours also.* When Christ destroyed the power of Satan, that victory was *also ours.* Jesus did not do all this for Himself. He did it for His Bride-to-be, the Church. Jesus became flesh and blood so that He could enter the battle with Satan. This was not for His sake, but *for the sake of the Church.* Because of this we are stronger than Satan. He can lord it over us *no more.* His rule over us ended at

Calvary. He does not have the rule over us anymore. We have been given power to rule over Satan! That is what it means to be seated with Christ.

Why Do We See Satan Still Fighting?

Even after we know who we are, we often forget. Satan knows what Christ did to him at Calvary. He also knows that the Church is seated with Christ in a ruling position. Yet, for all this, Satan carries on his battle against the Church. Satan does everything he can to keep the truth from the followers of Jesus. Satan does not want the Church to have any idea of their ruling power. Satan does what he can to make the followers of Jesus see themselves as weak and alone.

The attacks of Satan are not according to law (he has no right to do so), yet the Church must face them and win over them. God could, of course, put Satan completely out of the picture — do away with him. God has chosen, instead, to make use of him. While the devil exists, the Church is getting on-the-job training. If the devil were out of the way there would be no more battle, no more training for the Church. We are people in training. We want a place at the Marriage Supper of the Lamb. Unless we prepare, this is impossible. The crown is for him who wins. There is no winning without a battle. There is no battle without an enemy. Now we understand why God allows Satan to continue. Satan continues, however, for *only a limited time*.

A great danger is forgetting who we are. We are like the man James tells us about. This man looks at his face in a mirror, and after looking at himself he goes away and quickly forgets what he looks like (James 1:23–24).

Because we forget so easily we allow Satan to weigh us down. We forget that we are actually a part of Christ and that Satan is subject to us. It is very easy for us to fall back into living like we lived before — in fear and without hope. We must tell ourselves again and again that we are in Christ. Satan cannot touch Christ. We must tell Satan that he has no place in us. He cannot touch us.[2] "No one who has become a part of God's family makes a practice of sinning, for Christ, God's Son, holds him securely, and the devil cannot get his hands on him" (1 John 5:18, *LB*).

Satan wants the believer to forget that he is risen and seated with Christ. Satan wants the Christian to forget that his enemies are under his feet. Are there still fears, sickness and limits? If we know what Christ has done for us, maybe we have forgotten. We need to take another look.

Declaring Who We Are

We need to tell ourselves over and over again, "Because I am a part of Christ, 'accepted in the Beloved,' I am as dear to the Father as He. Because I am a part of Christ, the Father loves me as much as He loves Christ (see John 17:23, 26). Because I am a part of Christ, I have His wisdom. Christ has become wisdom for us (see 1 Corinthians 1:30). Jesus shares *His* holy ways with me. God accepts me because of this. I am sharing in His divine nature. I am born of Him. The Head and Body are one. *I share in all that Christ is and does.*"

The purpose of God is to make us like His Son. God works first on character. He wants us to be like His Son in character. He also wants us to be like Him in power.

This is not only to be known in our minds, to be mentally accepted as our position, but it is to be practical, to be experienced in our day-to-day life. "For all who are led by the Spirit of God are sons of God. And so we should not be like fearful, cringing slaves, but we should behave like God's very own children. . . . And since we are his children, we will share his treasures — for all God gives to his Son Jesus is now ours too. But if we are to share his glory, we must also share his suffering" (Romans 8:14,17, *LB*).

The Possibilities of the Church Are Without Limits

All that we have said is to understand better what God wants for us. He wants us to walk in the same life, power and liberty as His Son walked in. "As the Father hath sent me, even so send I you" (John 20:21, *KJV*). This "even so" suggests that we are sent out in the same ways as Jesus was sent out. "Even so" suggests that the grace and faith that Jesus had, we may have too. "Even so" suggests a great open field of possibilities without limits. The raw materials of heaven, supplies of all kinds, are laid up for our use. These are all kept in store for us, ready at a single call from us. They were put there *for us*. "From the fullness of his grace we have all received one blessing after another" (John 1:16, *NIV*). "Christ's love is greater than any person can ever know. But I pray that you will be able to know that love. Then you can be filled with the fullness of God" (Ephesians 3:19). *The only limits there are are those we put on ourselves.* One saint realized this truth to the full. He walked right into heaven — Enoch in the Old Testament.

God has given us the keys of the kingdom. He does not force us to use them. God waits. The rest is up to us, His Church! In His victory, Christ has given us the necessary weapons. It is up to us to use them. Our rank in heaven will depend on how we use our weapons.

NOTES

1.   When Jesus cried, "It is finished," it was the end or the completing of the demands of the law. "We owed a debt because we broke God's laws. That debt listed all the rules we failed to follow. But God forgave us that debt. He took away that debt and nailed it to the cross. God defeated the spiritual rulers and powers. With the cross God won the victory and defeated them. He showed the world that they were powerless" (Colossians 2:14–15).

2.   Job 1:9–12 shows that Satan cannot touch a child of God unless God permits him to do so. He is entirely under the control of God. Satan cannot touch us except God in love permits him to do so. The end result — as for Job, so for the tested believer: the blessing is always "twice as much" (Job 42:10).

7

THE MYSTERY OF PRAYERS THAT ARE NOT ANSWERED

We can come to God with no doubts. This means that when we ask God for things (and those things agree with what God wants for us), then God cares about what we say. God listens to us every time we ask him. So we know that he gives us the things that we ask from him (1 John 5:14–15).

These verses of Scripture declare that when God hears a prayer He also answers it. Our prayer really starts with God in the first place. It is God who put the prayer-thought in our hearts. Naturally, then, God is interested in answering that prayer. So, we can say, God has promised to answer all prayers that are according to His will. Therefore we can also say, "My prayer is according to the will of God; therefore He has answered my prayer."

Why? Why? Why?

In the light of this promise, and many others like it in the Bible, there is a question that troubles us: "Why should there ever be prayers that seem to have no answer?" We believe that Satan has been stripped of his power and his weapons. He has actually been "destroyed." We believe that the Church has been lifted up and given a high place, joined with Christ on His throne. We believe that the enemies of the Church have been put under her feet. We believe that the Church has power over her enemies. We believe she is acting in the name of her Lord, to bring about His will on the earth. Why is her victory not more clearly seen?

Selfish Reasons for Our Prayers?

It must be settled, once for all, that God is not at fault when our prayers do not seem to be answered. Most Bible writers teach that all prayers prayed according to the will of God will be answered. Neither Jesus nor John admit such a thing as a prayer not being answered. "Continue to ask, and God *will* give to you. Continue to search, and you *will* find. Continue to knock, and the door *will* open for you" (Matthew 7:7–8). "And if you ask for anything in my name, *I will do it for you*. Then the Father's glory will be shown through the Son. If you ask me for anything in my name, *I will do it*" (John 14:13–14). (Also 1 John 5:14–15 at the head of this chapter.)

Even though these promises are very clear and simple, yet there is something said in the Bible about prayer not being answered. James speaks of this, and he lays the fault on the human side. "Or when you ask, you do not receive because the reason you ask is wrong. You want things only so that you can use them for your own pleasures" (James 4:3).

Paul Made a Request But It Was Refused

Paul reports his own case of a prayer that was not answered. He explains that the reason was on the human side. "But I must not become too proud of the wonderful things that were shown to me. So a painful problem [thorn in the flesh] was given to me. This problem is a messenger from Satan. It is sent to beat me and keep me from being too proud" (2 Corinthians 12:7). Paul goes on to say that he prayed the Lord three times to take it away but without success. The Lord refused, and for a reason.

Although this is the only case of its kind in the New Testament, it may point us to a truth that operates almost everywhere. Does it speak of that sin, so dangerous and deadly — a proud heart? That was the sin that caused Lucifer (now called Satan) to fall from his high place of honor. Pride of self was the sin that had such far-reaching effect, not only for humans but even for the earth itself. That was the sin that caused such terrible sadness and suffering for people of all ages.

If any person makes himself or anything else the center of his world, he has started to destroy himself. To understand this, let us continue to study Lucifer. Before his fall he was one of the most honored of all the angels. Read Isaiah 14 and Ezekiel 28 and you will see that Lucifer guarded the throne of God. He is called "the anointed cherub that covers," "full of wisdom and perfect in beauty." Being next to God Himself, says Ezekiel, his heart was lifted up (filled with pride) because of his beauty. Today we might say "it went to his head." Ezekiel 28:18 in *The Living Bible* reads: "You defiled your holiness with lust for gain; therefore I brought forth fire from your own actions and let it burn you to ashes." God had given Lucifer great gifts. However, Lucifer entertained the wrong thoughts about those gifts. He thought of them in too personal, too selfish a way. These thoughts made his heart proud. The wrong thoughts were his undoing. The fire within him, started by his pride, "burned him to ashes." This is the general way of those who destroy themselves due to pride. Paul recognized this danger and he spoke to young Timothy about it. Paul said that a bishop must not be someone new in the faith, for he might have too high an opinion of himself. "Then he would be judged guilty for his pride just as the devil was" (1 Timothy 3:6).

Satan tries to produce the "Lucifer character" in every believer. He knows it will bring the believer under the same judgment he himself will suffer. Self-regard (that is, too high an opinion of oneself) is from the devil. It is a tool the devil often uses. Paul recognized this and knew that it was a danger for him also. He was in danger of thinking too highly of himself because God had given him such great eye-openers (2 Corinthians 12:7). Certainly few Christians have ever been carried to heaven and shown the things that Paul was shown. This was very wonderful for Paul, but there was also a danger. Would his heart become proud? That was the danger. Paul was given a "thorn," that is, some kind of problem. He asked

God to take it away. God did *not* take it away. Why? It was the means that God used to protect Paul against pride.

Spiritual Pride Stops the Working of the Lord

Few people, if any, have the experience that Paul had. Yet there is something for all of us to learn from his experience. Very few can take honors from the world or from God without becoming proud. Even a rather small taste of success can make us proud. There is always danger.

There are many different ways of falling into the sin of pride. Some of us have told of an answer to prayer in such a way that we get the credit for it. Then we say, "To God be the glory." But there is no glory left for God, for we have taken it all. Satan and his helpers know that human beings are very weak in this matter of pride. So, for this reason, they attack on this point. C.S. Lovett says these workers for Satan hide "just outside your skin" and take advantage of every weakness of the human race.

Who knows how much God would do for His servants if only it was safe for us! Even if a person says nothing about the honor he receives, often he will hold it carefully in his thoughts and take too much pleasure from it — a selfish kind of pleasure. One needs special grace from God in order not to fall into the class of the proud. This is such a great danger that often God does not dare to honor us the way He would like to. He wants to protect us from the sin of pride.

Does this mean that God has changed His mind about the promises He made? No, but it does mean that human weakness can slow up the answer that He is wanting to give us. (He has already prepared it, and is holding it for us.) God refused the request that Paul made in order to protect him from pride. Might this not explain why our prayers at times wait so long for an answer? History records a great many people who spoiled their own witness due to pride. Watchman Nee says that the great work that God must do in us is to help us see how small we really are. God is looking for a broken spirit in His children. God is interested in our characters. Some prayers have to wait so that the whole purpose of God can come to pass. God is at work perfecting our characters.

At times answers to prayers for healing wait for this same reason. Paul may have been asking for a healing (we are not sure of the nature of his problem) but he was refused. "Lest I be exalted." God was protecting Paul. Possibly God is also protecting us.

Failing to Pray (or Quitting) Stops the Working of the Lord

In earlier chapters we have said that God has given His children the right to rule over Satan. This truth is joined with the practice of believing prayer. This whole wonderful plan will not work in any shape or form without prayer. If God acted without prayer it would spoil His program of on-the-job training. The whole system of prayer was planned for just that — on-the-job training. There is no power or value in prayer as such. Really, prayer is the expressing of a need, of weakness. It is declaring that we cannot do it ourselves. God is able to do anything He wants to do. He does not need our prayers. All power starts with God and belongs to Him alone. *God is using prayer as a means of preparing His Church to rule in future days*. This will be after the Marriage Supper of the Lamb.

The Church needs to understand this and cooperate with the prayer program. This is the only way to win the battle with Satan while here on earth. The Church becomes strong as she battles with Satan. The Church will not experience the pleasure of ruling unless she continues in the practice of prayer. She must not give up.

Many People Organize — Few People Pray

The less the Church prays, the less results she will see. God is waiting for His Church to cooperate with him through prayer before He will work. Failing to pray *(really* pray) is often the reason for not getting answers. "You have not because you ask not." In earlier chapters we said that the social order has been kept from complete breakdown because of the prayers of Christians. There are few who read this who will not stop to consider their own habits regarding prayer. There are few who will feel they have measured up to the example of our Lord when it comes to prayer. In these times of ours are there men to compare with David Brainerd, Praying Hyde, Father Nash and E. M. Bounds? These were all men of strong and continuing prayer. (It is, of course, not good to compare or measure ourselves one with another.) Also we hear of much prayer in Asia, Africa, South America, Indonesia and the Soviet Union. Yet in the case of many people, little or nothing is happening because there is so little prayer.

Church Programs Instead of Prayer

Many churches have programs of education, Sunday Schools, Bible Schools, etc. They may have youth programs and be socially active. They may have Bible Camps. They may have teacher training classes. They may have big gospel meetings. They may even have a good program of giving. These are all fine in themselves. However, we ask, are they doing damage to the kingdom of Satan? The answer to that is, only if they were started by the leading of the Lord. What does God see as He looks at these programs? Does He own them? No doubt He would say of many of them, "I do not know you." Activity without prayer does no damage to the works of darkness.

Prayer Is Where the Action Is

John Wesley was right when he said, "God does nothing but in answer to prayer." Also S. D. Gordon said, "Prayer is striking the winning blow — service is gathering up the results." He was right. E. M. Bounds was also right when he said, "God shapes the world by prayer. God uses the prayers of His children to carry out His work in the world." Yes, prayer is where the action is!

Israel and Amalek

This fact is clearly seen by the battle between Israel and Amalek. God had brought Israel out of Egypt and was leading her towards the promised land. God was doing this in order to develop the nation of Israel. Satan was at work at that time too, and he tried to stop the forming of that nation. Satan stirred up the nation of Amalek (from the family line of Ishmael) to fight against

Israel. "So Moses said to Joshua, 'Choose some men and go and fight the Amalekites. Tomorrow I will stand on the top of the hill. I will hold the stick God gave me to carry.' Joshua obeyed Moses and went to fight the Amalekites. At the same time Moses, Aaron and Hur went to the top of the hill. As long as Moses held his hands up, the Israelites would win the fight. But when Moses put his hands down, the Amalekites would win" (Exodus 17:9–11). You know the rest of the story. When Moses was tired and had to rest his arms, Aaron and Hur stood on either side and held up his arms. They did this until Amalek gave up and Israel won. The plan God had for the nation of Israel made progress.

A Mountaintop Victory

Anyone hearing about this victory would likely give credit to the soldiers on the battlefield. But those of us who have read the story in the Bible know the real victory was on the prayer mountain. The real victory was with Moses and Aaron and Hur who held up the rod of God, the sign of His power. The Amalekites were tools of Satan. They were controlled by Satan. When the three praying people on the mountain kept praying in faith, the forces that drove the Amalekites became weak. They no longer had the power to win. In this way the Israelites won. When Moses got so tired he could no longer hold up his hands, the Amalekites won. Then Aaron and Hur came to help Moses. The two men held up his hands. This went on until the day was done.

It is said that Joshua won the battle. However, the real action was on the top of the mountain. The wicked spirits were brought under control there on the mountain. The winning blow was struck on the top of the mountain. Joshua and Israel were only gathering up the results. So we see that prayer is where the action is.

Since this is so, then what great opportunity the praying people have! They are on the front lines! Their work is equal to or greater than that of the pastor, the Christian worker, or the missionary. Their weapons are as useful as those of the very best of Christian leaders. As S. D. Gordon has said, "Prayer puts one in touch with a planet. I can as really be touching hearts for God in far away India or China through prayer as though I were there." He goes on to say, "A man may go aside today, and shut his door, and as really spend a half hour in India for God . . . as though he were there in person" *(Quiet Talks On Prayer)*. In other words, prayer has no limits when it comes to space or place. This is why Alexander Maclaren said, in speaking of the mission field, "Much prayer for the cause by those at the home base means much power on the field, and weakness at the home end means weakness on the field."

Prayer — Not Personal Power

Some people are very gifted. Does this mean they will be able to set another person free from the chains of Satan? NO! Some people are very loving and kind. Does this mean they will be able to set another person free from the chains of Satan? NO! Some people are great and powerful speakers. Does this mean they will be able to set another person free from the chains of Satan? NO! God may use such gifts, but in themselves there is not the power to set a single person free from the chains of Satan. "The flesh counts for nothing."

Prayer — Not Powerful Speaking

As heaven considers all things, spiritual victories are won in the secret place of prayer. The only power that is stronger than Satan and can set a prisoner free is the Holy Spirit. The only power that brings the Holy Spirit down to earth is *believing prayer*. Thank God for the gifts He has given to men. Thank God for men who can preach like Billy Graham. The power that has changed the lives of thousands of people, however, is not the power of great preaching. Rather, it is the power that has been set loose in the earth through the many prayers of the people of God. The prayer that goes up for Billy Graham and his meetings explains the great results. The wicked ones who fight against Billy Graham lose their power in the same way that Amalek lost his power in the battle against Israel. There were three praying men who kept right at the praying until the battle was won.

Prayer — Not Skill

Many gifted people appear on TV and radio. Of course it is important that they be trained to do their work well. The best of them, however, cannot bring freedom to a lost soul. This is the work of the Holy Spirit. It is brought down from heaven by true believing prayer. This same thing can be said about the message of a book. The writer does need to know the art of writing, true. The message, however, is locked within the pages until the Holy Spirit opens it and gives light to the reader. Here again we see how important prayer is. PRAYER IS WHERE THE ACTION IS.

Prayer and Reward

Some people think they should have gone to the mission field. For one reason or another they never went, and they worry about this matter. There is good news for them. If they will enter into the work of true prayer, they can do as much good or more than if they had gone to the mission field. There are people who say, "I really have no gifts." Others say, "I am sick, and there is nothing I can do." These peole do not have to miss out on the rewards. PRAYER IS WHERE THE ACTION IS! "Whoever meets a prophet and accepts him will receive the reward of a prophet. And whoever accepts a good man because that man is good will receive the reward of a good man" (Matthew 10:41). If receiving a person into your home will bring such a reward, then surely a prayer life will have its rewards.

No Room for Self-pity

This leaves no room for self-pity. Neither does it leave room for wishing you had the gifts of another person. Heaven has a book where records are kept. The name of every Christian is written in that book and his records are there too. This includes the famous people and those whose names are known only to their families and friends. In that book every person is important. The rewards are given out according to the records. How has a person handled the gift he has been given? No one will be judged according to the gift of another. Has a person been called to prayer? If he continues in faith the results will surprise everyone. The results may be even greater than those of the famous Christian leaders. It is true, "The future state of the world is in the hands of nameless saints."

The Prayer of Daniel

We see this truth in the book of Daniel, chapter 10. Again the nation of Israel was in view. Daniel had been fasting for three weeks. Towards the end of that period God gave Daniel a look into the future — a vision. The three-week period had been a time of sorrow for Daniel. The sorrow was about the people of Israel for whom he was praying. He was praying about their future. At last an angel appeared to Daniel with a message from heaven. The angel told Daniel why he had been delayed and this surprised Daniel (and us). God had heard his prayer the very day Daniel started praying. God also sent a messenger with the answer the very day that Daniel started praying. The messenger, however, was stopped on the way. *The Living Bible* puts it this way: "That very day I was sent here to meet you. But for twenty-one days the mighty Evil Spirit who overrules the kingdom of Persia blocked my way. Then Michael, one of the top officers of the heavenly army, came to help me, so that I was able to break through these spirit rulers of Persia" (Daniel 10:12–13).

Battle in the Spirit World

This is a true account of a real battle in the realm of the spirit. It is, no doubt, only one of many such battles that go on all the time in the spirit world. It is a story of action on two levels. Down by the river a man is fasting and praying. He labors, he begs, he continues to pray, he battles in prayer, he argues, he suffers in his praying. He sorrows day after day. He has read the words of Jeremiah and so he knows that the seventy years of living under a foreign power will soon be over. Those unhappy times for Israel are coming to an end. Of course God could make that all work out by Himself, but He did not choose to do it that way. Daniel realized that he himself had something to do with the future of his people. The prayer that Daniel prayed was part of the way God worked. God had been looking for a man who was willing to pray. He found the man — Daniel. A man who is self-centered cannot pray that kind of prayers, the kind that cooperates with God in His big plans.

As always, *God made the decision in heaven. A man was called to put that decision into effect on earth. That man would do this by means of prayer.* That part of the battle — the prayer times by the river — we understand. We can watch it. The other level of prayer battle we cannot watch. It is in the spirit world. While Daniel was praying on the earth, another battle was going on in heavenly places. Two angels, and possibly spirit forces under their direction, were locked in a strong fight that continued for three weeks. Since God cooperates with the prayers of His children, it is good that Daniel did not give up praying. If Daniel had given up, would God have had to look for another praying person? Probably so. Or would that prayer not have been answered? The victory was won down by the river bank, in the place of prayer. The action leading to decision and victory was there.

Why Keep On Keeping On?

This Bible story teaches us something else about prayer. As we look further into it, we may find the reason behind many of our unanswered prayers. Since our promise in 1 John, chapter 5, is true, every prayer prayed in faith, according to the will of God, is always answered in heaven. This verse says so. Satan, however, will not let an answer reach earth if he can help it. God hears our prayers right away. Then why do we have to keep on praying? *It is clear, we do not keep on praying to make God willing to answer. He is more than willing to answer. We keep on praying to overcome the spirits that battle against us. This is part of our on-the-job training.* If God took the matter out of the hands of the Church, there would be no way for the Church to become strong and able. That would not allow her to grow to full size. There would be no way for her, then, to become perfect. This helps us understand that we must pray and not give up. Many prayers may have been granted in heaven, but the person who prayed them gave up before the answer reached earth.

Jesus tells us about a man who needed three loaves of bread from his neighbor. His neighbor gave him the bread, but not until he saw that his friend would not be denied. Jesus finished His story with, "Ask, and keep on asking, and it shall be given you; seek, and keep on seeking, and you shall find; knock, and keep on knocking, and the door shall be opened to you" (Luke 11:9, *AMP*). The word from God to Habakkuk the prophet fits here: "The vision has its own appointed hour, it ripens, it will flower; if it be long then wait, for it is sure, and it will not be late" (Habakkuk 2:3, *Moffatt*). Let us not stop our praying. Mix with it strong desire. *How can we say that God does not answer prayer if we have not waited for it?*

On this point S. D. Gordon, in his *Quiet Talks on*

Prayer, says, "It is a 'fight to the finish.' Satan has trained and planned. He is not one to give up. He fights for his very life. He will not admit that he has lost the battle until he has to. . . . The enemy yields only when he must. He yields only what is taken from him by force. Therefore, the ground must be taken step by step. Satan continually returns to attack; therefore the ground must be held in the name of Jesus, the *Victor*" (paraphrased). "That is why you need to get God's full armor. Then on the day of evil you will be able to stand strong. And when you have finished the whole fight, you will still be standing. So stand strong, with the belt of truth tied around your waist. And on your chest wear the protection of right living" (Ephesians 6:13–14). *It is a battle of the wills.* The will of Satan and the will of the Christian — who will win? The Christian has the advantage because all the power of God is on his side. *If a Christian believes in God and keeps on praying there is no way he can lose the battle.*

Why Do We Pray So Little?

So far we have talked about why it seems that some prayers are not answered. God has given us strong promises about prayer. He is doing everything necessary to get us to pray. He told us He would answer. Jesus gave us lessons about prayer. He also was our example of a praying person, and we say that we are His followers. Why is it, then, that we pray so little? There may be many reasons, but probably the main one is *we do not really believe things will happen like the Word says they will.* We never really feel like we can depend on the Word. The Word says, "Continue to ask, and God *will* give to you. Continue to search, and you *will* find. Continue to knock, and the door *will* open for you" (Matthew 7:7). If we really and truly believed that, we would make prayer the main business of our lives. Failing to believe is the greatest cause of our "little praying." This failing is very deep in the human heart. Often it is not recognized. However, when we seldom pray we must admit that we really do not believe God. Anyone who believes those wonderful promises will pray.

The Worth of the Word

We need to consider the Word and give it its true worth. According to Erich Sauer in *The King of the Earth,* the spiritual nature of man expresses itself in the power of speech. "Speech is the direct way a man has of showing what is within him. Thought is the speech of the spirit. The spoken or written word forms a body for the thought. Speech is the instrument that lets people see the spirit" (paraphrased). Your thought is you. "For as he [a man] thinks in his heart, so is he" (Proverbs 23:7, *AMP*); this verse teaches that thought is a very important part of a person. That being true, then speech also is a very important part of a person, because it is the body of thought. From this we understand that the Word of God is a part of Himself. We understand that God Himself lives in His Word.

We must recognize, of course, in the truest sense, that Jesus Christ is the Word. He is the Word who was with the Father in the beginning (John 1:1). He is spoken of as the *Logos* or Word because it is He who perfectly shows us the Father. "No man has ever seen God. But God the only Son is very close to the Father. And the Son has shown us what God is like" (John 1:18).

We today, however, do not have the Word living among us in the flesh. But we do have His equal, the Comforter whom He sent, the Holy Spirit (John 16:7). The Holy Spirit caused the Word of God (the Bible) to be written. "All Scripture is given by God and is useful for teaching and for showing people what is wrong in their lives. It is useful for correcting faults and teaching how to live right. Using the Scriptures, the person who serves God will be ready and will have everything he needs to do every good work" (2 Timothy 3:16–17). God used human people to do the writing, but it is really the Word of God. This written Word of God forms a body for the thought of God. The written Word is not just "words" but truths given by the breath of God Himself. It is therefore *alive* (Hebrews 4:12), a "body" for the Holy Spirit. In a sense it is truly a part of God Himself. God lives in His Word.

We do not have Jesus with us in the flesh today. However we do have His Word. *What Jesus was in the flesh, His Word is to us today.* The power that is in Jesus is also in His Word. The written Word carries the same power as His spoken Word. *The living Word on the lips of a follower of Jesus (a true follower, living a holy life) has the same power as if Jesus were speaking it.* That is why, all over the world, true believers are seeing great results, even signs and wonders. There is power in the Word of God.[1]

God is the author of the Word. He also gives it its power. You cannot separate God from His Word. This is why Jesus could say, "Scripture is always true" (John 10:35). Because it is God-breathed it cannot fail. If God would not keep His Word that goes out of His mouth, He would not be God.

A Cure for Our "Little Praying"

Let us give the Word of God its proper place. Let us recognize our Lord in that Word. "God is not a man. He will not lie. God is not a human being. He does not change his mind. What he says he will do, he does. What he promises, he keeps" (Numbers 23:19). "I am watching to make sure my words come true" (Jeremiah 1:12). The writer of the letter to the Hebrews declares that it is impossible for God to lie (Hebrews 6:18). In John 10:35 Jesus Himself states clearly, leaving no room for doubt, "and Scripture is always true." He also said, showing His complete trust in the Scriptures, "Those are the same Scriptures that tell about me" (John 5:39). He said, "Your teaching is truth" (John 17:17). David puts the Word in the highest place when he says in Psalm 138:2, "You [God] have made your name and your word greater than anything." God is united with His Word. He has promised us this. *If the Church really and truly begins to believe the Word of God, it will cure the "little praying."*

Success of Perfect Faith

Prayer prayed according to the will of God will be answered. There are two things that can get in the way and stop it, but both of them can be handled so the result will be victory. The enemy of our souls, Satan, does all he can to stop the answers from coming to us. We, the Christians, can also stop our own prayers. The fault is never on the side of our Lord. "No! God will continue to be true even when every person is false" (Romans 3:4).

"God does not lie" (Titus 1:2). "And Scripture is always true" (John 10:35). *Faith will not be perfected until we take on ourselves the blame. There is failing on the human side. We need to admit that and make the necessary changes so that our prayers can be answered.* "According to your faith be it unto you" (Matthew 9:29, *KJV*). "Jesus answered, 'I tell you the truth. If you have faith, and do not doubt, you will be able to do what I did to this tree. And you will be able to do more. You will be able to say to this mountain, "Go, mountain, fall into the sea." And if you have faith it will happen'" (Matthew 21:21). "So I tell you to ask for things in prayer. And if you believe that you have received those things, then they will be yours" (Mark 11:24). "All things are possible for him who believes" (Mark 9:23). It is clear, *Jesus does not admit such a thing as unanswered prayer.* Shall we follow Him in this?

NOTES

1. There are many reports about the great working of God in Indonesia in 1965. Some who were eyewitnesses (and shall we not believe an eyewitness?) say that wonderful signs and wonders were done even by very simple people. Many of them could neither read nor write. This makes us think of Jesus' words, "I thank you, Father, Lord of heaven and earth, because you have hidden these things from the people who are wise and smart. But you have shown them to those who are like little children" (Luke 10:21). What blessings we may be losing. Do we consider ourselves advanced in religious matters and yet have never experienced the wonders of His working?

8

THE PROBLEM OF FAITH

"If you can!" All things are possible for him who believes (Mark 9:23).

The problem of a living faith, of faith without doubt, is a very real one. Even many people who have regular habits of prayer are still troubled with doubt. Many people pray and pray without arriving at the sense that their prayers are heard. They do not break into the joy of knowing that the answer is on the way. What can be done to change this?

Praise Is the Answer

There has been much teaching on prayer, but little on praise. Now in our day, however, God is raising up leaders to teach the Church how to praise. The Bible speaks more on praise than on prayer. In the Bible we find that the whole universe and everything in it join together in a wonderful song of praise to God. This includes all living beings as well as the world of nature. Notice especially Psalms 148–150. Psalm 145:10 declares that "Lord, everything you have made will praise you. Those who belong to you will bless you." *Praise is the highest work of the angels. Heaven is one grand note of praise.* The angels worship Him without stopping. "Each of these four living things had six wings. The living things were covered all over with eyes, inside and out. Day and night they never stop saying: 'Holy, holy, holy is the Lord God All-Powerful. He was, he is, and he is coming'" (Revelation 4:8). "Then I looked, and I heard the voices of many angels. The angels were around the throne, the four living things, and the elders. There were thousands and thousands of angels — there were ten thousand times ten thousand. The angels said in a loud voice: *'The Lamb who was killed is worthy* to receive power, wealth, wisdom and strength, honor, glory and praise!'" (Revelation 5:11–12). "Then I heard what sounded like a great many people. It sounded like the noise of flooding water and like loud thunder. The people were saying: *'Hallelujah! Our Lord God rules.* He is the All-Powerful'" (Revelation 19:6). Surely that which takes up all the time in heaven ought to take up some of our time here on earth!

Practical Sides of Praise

For some reason the Church as a whole has not realized the importance of praise. Many people think it is a beautiful exercise but of little practical value. However, if praise is so important to the angels, there must be a reason for it. If the song of praise never ends in heaven (Revelation 4:8), it must be of great worth. Would God allow something to go on in heaven if it would have no use — no value? We will look at some of the practical values of praise.

Praise Develops Character

If the highest work of angels is praise, might it not also be the highest work of the human spirit? To come closer and closer to the character of God is the very highest good that a human being can hope for. This is the greatest thing, the highest joy, the greatest pleasure of the human spirit. Some people are very angry with God, hating Him and speaking evil of Him. This strengthens the spirit of Satan within them. On the other hand, there are people who give thanks to God. They honor Him with songs of praise and worship. This strengthens the godly spirit within them. Step by step, they go from glory to glory, always more like the God they serve. We can expect this process to go on forever and ever. It starts on earth, it continues in heaven. So we see that praise will help us reach the very desire that is most precious to us — becoming like God. God is at work "bringing many sons to glory."

Praise and a Healthy Mind

The subject of a healthy mind has caught the attention of many people in our times. It is reported in the world at large that half of the hospital beds are filled with people who are troubled in their minds. Great hospitals and care centers have been built to help these people. This is an important branch of medical care, the study of psychiatry. It is my opinion that a big program of praise and worship would put many psychiatrists out of work and empty a great many hospital beds.

Self-centeredness — that is, always thinking of oneself — is the cause for most of the nervous problems in our world. A person who always thinks of himself becomes, in time, angry. Then he tries to defend himself against all others. He begins to hate all people and he behaves in such ways that he loses all his friends. When a person becomes completely self-centered he destroys himself. Jesus explained it this way: "Whoever wants to save his life will lose it. And whoever gives his life for me will save it" (Luke 9:24).

Praise Takes Our Thoughts Off Ourselves

This is one of the greatest values of praise: we get our minds off ourselves. Praise and worship demand that Jesus becomes our center and not we ourselves. It is impossible to praise while we are thinking about ourselves. When praise becomes a way of life, our precious Lord becomes the center of our worship. In this way the life of a person is made whole. There is a healing of the mind and the nervous system. Praise helps us forget ourselves and that brings health.

Praise Is Not a Costly Thing

Some people pay a great deal of money to see a psychiatrist (a doctor of the mind) and yet find no help for their problem. If a Christian is suffering from severe sadness of spirit there is another way for him. He can turn to his loving, healing Father in heaven. If he continues to pray and praise, healing will begin. Praise is a practical and rewarding exercise.

Praise and Peace in the Home

The home is attacked in many ways. Sharp words often destroy the peace of the home. Self-pity attacks some members of the family. Sharp words and praise do not belong together. Neither do self-pity and praise. If the members of the family begin and continue to praise God, watch and see what happens to sharp words and self-pity. The practice of praise will raise the spiritual tone of any family.

An Example From the Bible

There is so much said about praise in the Bible. This is not surprising, for praise is a very important subject. *Satan fears praise even more than prayer.* We understand that by the story in 2 Chronicles chapter 20. A group of nations, Moab, Ammon and others, declared war on Jehoshaphat, the king of Judah. King Jehoshaphat called for a day of fasting, praying and sorrowing. Israelites from all over the country gathered in Jerusalem. Jahaziel, the prophet of God, told Jehoshaphat (the king) that there would be victory without a single battle. This is described in verses 20–22: "Jehoshaphat's army went out into the Desert of Tekoa early in the morning. As they were starting out, Jehoshaphat stood and said, 'Listen to me, people of Judah and Jerusalem! Have faith in the Lord your God. Then you will stand strong. Have faith in the Lord's prophets. Then you will succeed.' Jehoshaphat listened to the people's advice. Then he chose men to be *singers* to the Lord.

They were to *praise* the Lord because He is holy and wonderful. They marched in front of the army. They said, *'Thank the Lord. His love continues forever.'* As they began to sing and praise God, the Lord set ambushes. He set them for the people of Ammon, Moab and Edom. They were the ones who came to attack Judah. And they were defeated.''

An Army Destroyed Themselves

Why did praise have such a good effect in this story? It was because this was a battle in the heavenly places, *a battle between good and evil spirits*. As always, Satan purposed to destroy the nation of Israel and so destroy the coming King, the Lord Jesus. So it was Satan who caused the group of kings to fight against King Jehoshaphat. The prayer-and-praise program of the king did more harm to the enemy than the army could have done. This program was supported by a nationwide time of fasting and prayer. The praise of the singers and the stirring of the Lord gave the enemy much trouble. They were no longer able to think clearly. They behaved like men who had lost their minds. They were filled with such fear that they behaved completely without reason. They turned on one another and destroyed their own army.

Why Does Praise Have Such an Effect on Satan?

Mrs. Frances Metcalf, in her little book *Making His Praise Glorious,* has spoken on certain verses in Scripture regarding this. In Psalm 80:1, 99:1 and Isaiah 37:16 we find that "He [God] sits between the gold creatures with wings." When we read about the tabernacle in the Old Testament we find that figures of these cherubim [heavenly beings] covered the Ark. This special box was in the place called the Holy of Holies. Those forms [cherubim] over the Ark speak to us about the real heavenly beings that are around the throne of God. Night and day they cry, "Holy, holy, holy, Lord God Almighty." That is the place where one finds God. He is right there, in the center of that great burst of praise.

Praise and the presence of God have a great attraction for one another. True, God is everywhere. However, His power to bless and gladden hearts is stronger in some places than in others. In the center of praise God is powerfully active and His influence is very great on those busy with praising. In Psalm 22:3 we are told that God "inhabits the praises" (*KJV*) of His people. This means that where there is praise that He can accept, *there He is*. He will let us know that He is with us. *And His presence always drives away the devil.* Satan cannot bear to stay in His presence. Many people have known that there was power in praise, but they could not explain it. It may well be because Satan has been put out — therefore the power of God is at work. Satan finds it impossible to work where the influence of God is so strong.[1]

The secret of overcoming faith, then, is *praise*. It was James who said, "So give yourselves to God. Stand against the devil, and the devil will run away from you" (James 4:7). Praise produces the kind of state where God lives. So we see that praise defends us well against the attacks of Satan. There is no weapon so powerful to use against Satan as praise. Praise brings victory in prayer.

It Is Important to Continue With Much Praise

It is not enough to praise now and then, when we feel like it. *We need to make it our habit, our way of life.* "I will praise the Lord at all times. His praise is always on my lips" (Psalm 34:1). "Happy are the people who live at your Temple. They are always praising you" (Psalm 84:4). It has been pointed out that in heaven praise is so important that a certain order of beings do nothing else — they praise God day and night (Revelation 4:8). King David knew that praise was important. Like the praising ones in heaven, King David set aside an army of four thousand Levites to do nothing else but to praise the Lord (1 Chronicles 23:5). One of the last things David did before he died was to organize a program of praise. Each morning and each evening a group of these four thousand Levites were busy with this service. "The Levites also stood every morning and gave thanks and praise to the Lord. They also did this every evening" (1 Chronicles 23:30). To the shame of the Church today this great program of praise has been almost forgotten.[2]

Praise as a Way of Life

How shall this life of praise have the greatest effect? Many people must be busy with it. It must be a fixed habit. It must go on and on. *It must be a full-time calling, a total way of life.* We see these thoughts in Psalm 57:7 (*KJV*): "My heart is *fixed,* O God, my heart is fixed; I *will* sing and give praise." This suggests that we have considered and decided to live a life of praise. "My heart is FIXED." This kind of life will take more than just a burst of praise when we feel especially happy. We are told that at the very time of writing this psalm, David was in hiding from Saul who wanted to kill him. Praise was more than a passing feeling with David. Praise had entered deeply into his spirit; it was a part of his very being. It had become "second nature" to David.

Praise for All Things

This order of praise is not always easy. It does not always rise up without effort. If everything is going well for us it is easy to praise. It is natural to praise for "good" things. It is normal to praise for success and good health. David, however, was praising when his life was in great danger. The Apostle Paul says that one is to "always give thanks to God the Father *for everything*" (Ephesians 5:20). This, therefore, must include things that are painful and that even seem evil.

The Real Reason Why We Should Praise Continually

The very character of God is the reason we should be forever praising. *He is worthy of praise.* Let us think for a moment what would have happened if Satan had succeeded in his battle with our Lord. Then the ruling one would have been total evil instead of total love. Instead of hell being limited to a certain place it would have been everywhere. Praise God, Satan lost! Today there is "a heart at the heart of the universe." "The hands that were nailed do move the wheels of human history and shape the happenings of each life" (Maclaren). As David said in Psalm 31:15, "My life is in your hands." Because Almighty Love is in power, far above all, those who are with Him are kept safely and "the Evil One can not hurt him" (1 John 5:18). *Nothing that is really evil can reach a child of God.* This is because Almighty Love works all things, both "good" and "evil," into final good. God turns things around. This even includes the mistakes of His own children.

Praise as an Offering to God

How can one offer this kind of praise? Hebrews 13:15 gives us a key: "Through Jesus, therefore, let us continually offer to God a sacrifice of praise — the fruit of lips that confess his name" (*NIV*). What is meant by the "sacrifice of praise"? A sacrifice (offering) calls for death. In the Old Testament service it was an animal that died. In the "sacrifice of praise" it is the "I," the "self" that must die. *A person must die to his own judgment and his own opinion of what is good or bad.* What is "the fruit of lips"? Our words. We express ourselves by our words. Our offering of praise to God is not complete until we express it *with our words*.

We have all had experiences which we would call "bad." That is, the results seemed to do only harm. Try as we would, it is very hard to be happy about those happenings. It is at times like these that we offer the "sacrifice of praise." That is the time we are called upon to die to our own way of thinking, our own opinions, our own choices, and our own judgment. That is the time to give praise to God with our lips. It is a sacrifice of praise.

The Faith Which Supports Continual Praise

Without faith we cannot offer the sacrifice of praise. It is a living faith in the Lord our God that lifts up the offering or sacrifice to God. We believe that He is good, and that He is able. "Be quiet and know that I am God"

(Psalm 46:10). This faith knows that things never "just happen" in this world. This faith knows that Satan is not going to pull a trick while God is "not watching," for He is the *all-seeing* One. This faith knows that God is able, that He has all power and that He is wiser than Satan. This faith knows that Satan is the loser in the long run.

Praise Removes the "Evil" From Any Condition

Satan was thrown out of heaven long ago. It is the devil that brings evil to people or places. He can likewise be thrown out of these places where he has settled. How? By praise, be it by one person alone or by a great gathering of Christian people. Are you in a difficult position? The poison, or evil, can be taken out of that position by praise. The condition does not always change, but as we continue to praise, we ourselves change.

God is interested in our hearts. As we change and become more like our Master, that is far more important than a change in our conditions. When we offer the "sacrifice of praise" we accept a certain position. We agree with God that nothing but good can happen to us, no matter how "evil" it may seem. This way of thinking helps us enter into a life or habit of praising at all times and places.

Praising for Cancer

Amy Carmichael said that the very center of a problem is not in the thing itself but in the way we receive and behave towards that problem. The problem itself passes. The way we have thought about it and acted on it remains as a part of us for this life and the next. Satan plans that our problems should drive us far from God. Satan wants us to question God and His actions. He wants us to think, "Is God really good?" He wants us to say, "Surely, if God were good, He would never allow this terrible thing to happpen."

When one accepts these thoughts he turns away from God and acts as an enemy of God. His character, then, begins to lose the ground he has gained. In this way Satan wins. If, instead, we turn to God in times of trouble, the opposite is true. If we can then say, "This will turn into good in the end," our character will grow and be strong. If such be our way of life, *God wins and Satan loses*. The problem will leave the one suffering from it a stronger person with greater knowledge of God and His ways. That is why a woman who had cancer could give a good witness. She had not been living close to God, but when she got sick, she sought His face. She said, at last, "I have been richly blessed by this cancer." It also gives light on the words of Alexander Maclaren: "Don't waste your sorrows." Watchman Nee also says that one does not learn anything new about God except through suffering.

Is not this God worthy of our praise? — one who can take all things, both bad and good, and turn them into good? — one who can make all the plans and workings of Satan to turn out to do Satan himself harm? A God with such a character is reason enough for us to obey the words in Ephesians 5:20: "Always give thanks to God the Father for everything, in the name of our Lord Jesus Christ."

> Ill that He blesses is our good,
> And unblest good is ill;
> And all is right which seems most wrong,
> If it be His sweet will.[3]

This, then, is the faith that a trusting child of God can have (Psalm 91:10).

Praise, the Secret of Faith Without Doubt

Mrs. Metcalf has said she believes that thanksgiving and praise is the way to victory in *all* our problems. This is a big statement, but it has both reason and Scripture to back it up. Satan is busy trying to make our prayers of no effect. When we get the better of Satan, our prayers *will be answered*. Let us not forget, prayer that succeeds results in *destroying* the purposes of Satan. The main part of prayer is *faith* — faith with a *note of victory!* That note of victory is *praise*. Let us *choose* to praise, fix praise into a *habit,* and make our praise *strong* and *active. Praise is the highest form of prayer!* Praise unites the asking to a glad faith! Praise is the sparkplug that gets faith going! Praise gives wings to our faith! Praise makes our faith pure and takes out the doubt!

The secret of answered prayer is faith without doubt (Mark 11:23). The secret of faith without doubt is *praise* — praise that is happy, that is strong, that is a way of life. *This order of praise is the answer to the problem of living faith and prayer that succeeds.*

NOTES

1. David Wilkerson, in one of his books, tells of an experience about praise. In the early part of his work, David met a group of street boys in New York City. As he came near them there were signs that the boys were planning to attack. David Wilkerson was looking to the Lord to guide him as he kept walking toward the boys. At the very moment when the boys looked ready to attack, David clapped his hands and shouted, "Praise the Lord!" The whole group broke rank and ran. How can this be explained? They were likely controlled by evil spirits and lost their nerve at the shout of praise. The evil spirits can never stand praise.

Let me give another account about the power of praise. A servant of the Lord was holding meetings in a certain church. In order to be alone for prayer this man went into a nearby field. He did not know that there was a dangerous bull in that very field. When he saw the bull charging he knew it was too late to run. The preacher thought his end had come. However, just before the bull reached him he shouted, "Praise the Lord!" The bull stopped in his tracks, turned around and ran.

How shall we explain this? The writer suggests that Satan sent evil spirits into the animal in order to destroy the minister and the work God was doing through him. The shout of praise was too much for the evil spirits. It was like when the enemies of Israel lost their senses as the children of Israel sang and praised.

2. The type of church that is growing the fastest today is the charismatic or Pentecostal church. Why is this? Many of the people from those churches say it is because they speak in new tongues. This,

they say, proves that they have been filled with the Holy Spirit.

Many, however, outside the movement — and some within — say there is another way to explain the great growth. They have discovered the secret of praise. Might this be at least part of the reason for their growth? They have added a period of praise and worship to their regular service. These churches have a time before the message when all the members join in strong praise to God. They raise their hands to heaven and worship together. This often results in a beautiful sense of the presence of the Holy One. It is like the songs on earth are flowing together and joining with the songs of heaven.

The author believes that it is this Scriptural way of worship, giving God the praise He has long been denied, that causes the church growth. Whether a church believes in speaking in tongues or not, there is no reason for its members not joining in praise to God.

3. NO SUCH THING AS BAD NEWS! Someone has said that there is no such thing as "bad news" for a Christian. It is only an opportunity to grow in faith. As we grow spiritually, God can trust us with bigger broblems! We go from one to another, getting stronger all the time. Let us think of a runner on a race track. Does he plead with his trainer to remove the difficulties? No, the track is planned to make the runner stronger and faster. God has given some great promises to those who keep on running until the race is over. He has given great promises to the winners. How can we win if there is nothing to win over? There are people and heavenly beings watching us as we run the race of life. What will they see? Will they hear us say, "Thank you, God. I know you are big enough and loving enough to help me face this new problem"? If so, the face of our Lord will light up with joy!

9

ORGANIZED ACTION

Evening, and morning, and at noon, will I pray, and cry aloud: and he shall hear my voice (Psalm 55:17, *KJV*).

Now you have almost finished this book. Has it changed your prayer life? Are you following a better prayer plan now than before? Do you spend more time in private prayer? Does your church have a more active prayer program than before you read this book? If your answer is "no" to all these questions, we fear this book has been of little or no value to you. *Satan does not care how many people read about prayer if he can keep them from praying.* When a church really believes that "prayer is where the action is," many things will happen. That church will give prayer the highest place in their program. Their most gifted people will organize a prayer program. They will give time to seeking the Lord in strong, lively prayer.

The prayer program of the church, of course, will depend on the private prayer program of the members of the church. If the members do not have a strong calling and desire to pray, neither will the church.

First Things First

Some people say they have no time to pray. All of us have the same amount of time in a twenty-four hour day. What you do with those twenty-four hours depends on your system of values. *There is always time for that which a person ranks of highest value.* We all take time to eat and sleep, work, take care of the children and make a home. These things take a lot of time, yet it is possible to make time for daily prayer as well. Those who manage to do this find it very rewarding.

Organizing Important Matters

There are 168 hours in a week. After a person works 40 hours a week, there are still 128 hours left. Allowing 56 hours for sleep still leaves 72 hours. Counting 21 hours per week for meals leaves 51 hours. It is hard to cut down on these hours. If we spend one hour a day with the Word of God and in prayer, we still have 44 hours for special, personal things — free time. Of course, there are some people like farmers and mothers where free hours are not possible. We only include this to give a little idea of time and how it can be managed.

Oftentimes old people and sick people have "nothing to do." They might like·to try spending several hours a day in prayer. That would be the brightest part of their day. They would know their lives were useful.

A Prayer Library

Each local church must decide the form and shape of their prayer program. This prayer program, however, MUST be the *most important business* of the entire church program, both for the group and for the members. Every church should also have a prayer library. There are many good books on the subject of prayer. The best of these books should be in the church library. Those by E. M. Bounds are among the best. *Quiet Talks on Prayer* by S. D. Gordon, *The Life and Diary of David Brainerd, Praying Hyde, The Kneeling Christian,* and *Rees Howells, Intercessor* — these are a few of the very best.

Suggestions to Help You Pray

Many churches have a prayer meeting in the middle of the week. That is a good place to start. Small groups praying in the homes is a good way to increase the praying. Ladies meeting together to pray, men doing the same, young people gathering to pray, all this gives variety to the prayer life. Some will gather before going to work in the morning, others will meet at lunch hour. Others will have an all-night of prayer or a half-night of prayer. There may be a week-end of prayer, or a few days spent together to pray.

It is better to start small and slowly increase the prayer time than to make plans so great that you cannot keep them up. For example, one night of prayer a month is a good way to start. One might add fasting to the prayer. Some churches have a prayer chain, where a different person prays each hour, around the clock. The

Moravians, who grew strong under the direction of Count Zinzendorf, carried on a prayer chain that lasted 100 years. This was the beginning of the modern missionary movement.

Many people use lists when they pray. In this way they will not forget to pray for different needs. *Helps to Intercession* by Andrew Murray is a useful prayer guide.

Each church must find the leading of the Lord as to what will fit their group best. *Remember: Only what is done by prayer and faith will produce true and lasting results.*

PRAYER IS WHERE THE ACTION IS; therefore, SET THINGS IN ORDER FOR PRAYING.

Here are two places where you can get prayer helps, both books to read and tapes to listen to:

Peter Lord
Park Avenue Baptist Church
2600 Park Avenue
Titusville, Florida 32780

Change the World Ministries
P.O. Box 5838
Mission Hills, CA 91345

The following material is included by special request of the author:

APPENDIX:

PRACTICAL PRAYING

by Dick Eastman, Director
Change the World Ministries
P.O. Box 5838
Mission Hills, CA 91345

"Prayer is the mightiest force in the world," wrote an atomic scientist several years ago. No statement could be more true.

Prayer brings the one who prays into union with the Ruler of all things. Besides this, it sends forth that same power into a world that needs changing, oh, so badly. For this reason Change the World Ministries is working hard to train those who are praying. One thing we do is to organize and carry on Change the World Schools of Prayer. You, too, can join this force. Do not wait about this important matter; write in today.

Sadly, many Christians fail to join the ranks of those praying people we call "world changers." This is because they have never learned to make their prayer life practical. To help you, we have added these few words to the book Paul Billheimer wrote.

To pray in this way a person needs two things: something to pray about and a quiet place to seek the Lord. Let us think about these two things.

How to Pray

God gives you 96 fifteen-minute time periods every day. Will you give God at least one or two of these time periods in prayer for your loved ones, friends, and the world? Some people do not answer this question because they say, "I want the Holy Spirit to lead me." If you ask those same people, "How much time did the Holy Spirit lead you to spend in prayer this last week?" they blush with shame. Indeed, why must we wait for a call when the Word of God cries out to all people of all times, "Never stop praying" (1 Thessalonians 5:17). So we have our call to pray. We now suggest some ways to help you in your prayer life.

First, divide your 15-minute prayer time into three periods, that is, five minutes each. You might like to spend the first five minutes in praise and worship of the Lord. Take time to love God because He is God. Remember, the way to enter the gates of heaven is to give thanks and praise (Psalm 100). After this you will be ready to pray for other needs.

Second, take five minutes to pray for needs that are close to you. That could mean prayer for your family as well as your local people. This would include your church and pastor. You will be surprised at how much can be included in a five-minute prayer time.

Finally, pray for specific countries of the world. (Change the World Ministries has Prayer Maps to send out to those who ask for them. You will see all the countries of the world, and their names on this map.) There are 210 countries. If you were to pray for all of those countries in five minutes, you would have time to do nothing more than to read off their names. We suggest that you divide 210 by 7 and you get 30. Pray for 30 countries each day, and in a week you will have prayed for the whole world.

But what can we pray about as far as these countries go? Most of them we hardly know about. First of all, we can pray as Jesus told us to pray — ask the Lord to send workers into these countries (Matthew 9:38). We should also ask God to save people in each country for He has said, "If you ask me I will give you the nations. All the people on earth will be yours" (Psalm 2:8). Further, pray that God will bless the efforts of those who distribute books and Christian articles. Ask God that He will bless the witness of the Christians in that country. You might like to pray like this: "Oh God, I lift Indonesia before you. Send some of your own workers into Indonesia. Bless those who are already there, busy at work. Let your Spirit be moving in the hearts of those who try to take your gospel into every home there in Indonesia."

You can pray a prayer like that in only 20 seconds. Yet you have called on God to bless all in that country. God honors prayers like that. In all this praying we must honor the Holy Spirit and listen for His leading. At times

He will make us stop and spend more time with a certain country. When you pray for Communist or Muslim countries pray especially for those in high government offices. Pray that they will get a change of heart. This will open doors for Christian workers to enter the country. It will give them freedom to work in that country.

In fact, Paul told his co-worker, young Timothy, to pray especially for "all who have authority" (1 Timothy 2:2). This includes kings, presidents, and all those who govern the affairs of the nations. We are to ask God to move on the hearts of these men in such a way that doors will open in their countries to spread the gospel. To help you in this kind of prayer we have prepared a special listing of all kings and presidents for every country in the world. There are few, if any, other mission organizations that offer such a prayer list. If you use it every day, you will be a "world changer." Be sure to write and ask for these helps. Say which helps you want. These helps include: the Prayer Map, a list of the kings and presidents, and a booklet called "15 Ways to Make Your Prayer Life More Meaningful."

Where to Pray

For several years I had realized the importance of prayer. One night God gave me the idea of a prayer center where young people from all over the country could come to pray. They would come prepared to give God a certain amount of time in prayer. During their year at that place, these people would pray for two hours or more, certain hours of each day, and then others would take their place to pray. The prayer would never stop night or day. The room where these people were to pray was to be called "The Gap." This was based on the words God spoke to Ezekiel, "I looked for a man among them who would build up the wall and stand before me in the gap on behalf of the land. . . ." (Ezekiel 22:30, *NIV*). Six months after I was exercised for this prayer center, God gave us such a place. For years, prayer has continued day and night in "The Gap." Here people pray for the needs of the world.

To the best of my knowledge, the first couple to begin such a gap prayer service as a result of our prayer center was a Baptist couple. Since then many people from different churches have written saying, "Add us to your 'gap' list! We have begun times of prayer in our home."

My wife Dee and I have started our own family gap ministry. We built a special family prayer place or "gap" in our backyard. We go in one by one, or sometimes our whole family gathers there to pray. It has changed my personal prayer life. Each day I pray for all the countries of the world. It is a happy sound to my ears when I hear our two young daughters beg us, "Let us go to pray in the 'gap.'" Our daughters, Dena and Ginger, want us to tell them about the different countries of the world, as we look at the map of the world.

To begin a gap prayer time one must simply set aside a room or closet especially for prayer. That room should not be a sewing room, nor an office, but a place set apart. Every member of our family knows it is a special place of prayer, our special "Gethsemane." We go there to be alone with God. I strongly suggest that all who read this start their own "gap" — their place of prayer. Think about this important matter.

Write to the address below and we will add your name to our list:

Change the World Ministries
P.O. Box 5838
Mission Hills, CA 91345

This book was produced by the Christian Literature Crusade. We hope it has been helpful to you in living the Christian life. CLC is a literature mission with ministry in over 40 countries worldwide. If you would like to know more about us, or are interested in opportunities to serve with a faith mission, we invite you to write to:

Christian Literature Crusade
P.O. Box 1449
Fort Washington, PA 19034